Rosenberg/Barthes/Hassan

The Postmodern Habit of Thought

Rosenberg

Barthes

Hassan

The Postmodern Habit of Thought
JEROME KLINKOWITZ
The University of Georgia Press
Athens and London

Paperback edition, 2012
© 1988 by the University of Georgia Press
Athens, Georgia 30602
www.ugapress.org
All rights reserved
Designed by Mary Mendell
Set in Sabon

Printed digitally in the United States of America

The Library of Congress has cataloged the hardcover
edition of this book as follows:
Klinkowitz, Jerome.
Rosenberg, Barthes, Hassan : the postmodern habit
of thought / Jerome Klinkowitz.
139 p. : ill. ; 24 cm.
Bibliography: p. [131]–134.
Includes index.
ISBN 0-8203-0997-4 (alk. paper)
1. Rosenberg, Harold, 1906–1978. 2. Barthes, Roland.
3. Hassan, Ihab Habib, 1925– . 5. Criticism—History—
20th century. 6. Postmodernism (Literature) I. Title.
PN98.P67 K55 1988
801'.95'0904—dc19   87-22195

Paperback ISBN-13: 978-0-8203-4016-6
         ISBN-10: 0-8203-4016-2

British Library Cataloging-in-Publication Data available

Title page: Richard Estes, "Paris Street Scene," 1972.
Collection of the Virginia Museum of Fine Arts,
Gift of Sydney and Frances Lewis.

for S.T.D., in memory

Contents

1. Rosenberg/Barthes/Hassan   1
2. Harold Rosenberg: Art as Act   13
3. Roland Barthes: To Write   43
4. Ihab Hassan: Re-visioning Man   93
5. The Postmodern Habit of Thought   121

Bibliography   131

Index   135

One

Rosenberg/Barthes/Hassan

What characterizes an era of aesthetics is its habit of thought. Scholars of neoclassic English literature say that to Dr. Samuel Johnson romanticism was literally unimaginable. In the later nineteenth century the doctrine for writing realistic fiction was based upon a mode of current scientific intelligence which believed the thing in itself could be isolated, something romanticism itself could not have fathomed. Intellectual concerns of a different order were at the core of modernistic belief, and in our own day postmodernism has distinguished itself by a polemical refusal, argued point by point, to accept these standards.

At the interface of such aesthetic eras one finds not just transition and transformation but also disruption, dissidence, and confusion. For all their apparent differences, systems of thought make poor material for contrast, as issues of personality always threaten to intrude. To catch the sense of a period, it might be more profitable to look at the thinkers themselves—to examine their habits of thought which diverge from the previous pattern, and consider the axioms which derive from such thinking. In the course of literary and aesthetic history, it seems that the figure of the thinker is more palpable than the fully abstract system of an age's thought.

A grasp of new systems is not impossible, but to see such thinking evolve within the aesthetic statements of working critics yields a more practical body of beliefs. When a number of such thinkers, from diverse backgrounds and devoted to an exceptionally wide range of cultural pursuits, coincide in the practice of their beliefs, it is worth comparing the nature of their work with an eye toward an emerging aesthetic. Harold Rosenberg, Roland Barthes, and Ihab Hassan are just such figures for study. Although nearly twenty years separate their births, all three come to prominence in the same era of social, ideological, and aesthetic turmoil framed by the 1960s. Each begins with a specific interest—art, semiotics, and literature respectively—only to look outward to larger cultural concerns, principally because their initial critical interest prompts a revolution in method and belief. Unhappy with the dictates of modernism and impatient with its lingering influence, each argues for a new way of seeing his subject. And as Harold Rosenberg disengages painting from its static memorialism, Roland Barthes deconstructs sign systems to show values in a new sense of fluidity, and Ihab Hassan reaches beyond the conventions of literature to shape a new vision of man, one can distinguish a style for which each has a different name. Rosenberg calls it the *more modern* modern, Barthes says *modernity,* and Hassan suggests the term *postmodernism,* but all three descriptions posit themselves against the modernism which so inhibits its thinkers.

Selecting the innovations of a major art critic, semiologist, and literary scholar which influence a common period makes for a fair cross section of aesthetic thought, but with Rosenberg, Barthes, and Hassan the ground covered is even more comprehensive. Rosenberg's background is that of the most familiar American intellectual, a Jewish-American critic born, raised, and working in New York. Roland Barthes, a French Protestant, is a stellar representative of the European intellectual community with traditions all its own. And Ihab Hassan, born in Cairo and having pursued an international education, remains today a representative of the cosmopolitan thinker, at home with literature or philosophy in the American Middle West, Europe, or the Far East. The anti-academic nature of their innovations makes them late to begin publishing, with Rosenberg's first book waiting until 1959 (at age 53), Barthes's appearing in 1953 (age 38) but not translated until 1967 (matching Rosenberg's age), and Hassan's in 1961 (age 36), but once on the scene their books multiply quickly in number and influence. Their initial, seminal works are published with the popular press, but by the late 1970s all three have their works issued or reprinted by leading university presses and are installed as distinguished professors in their countries' major academic institutions—a sign of the academy recognizing the permanent effect of their revolutionary work, as opposed to purely academic thought making its way out into the mainstream. The Horizon Press editions of Rosenberg's work, Barthes's publications with Seuil in France and Hill and Wang/Farrar, Straus and Giroux in the U.S., and the success of Hassan's first two books as Harper & Row and Knopf paperbacks signal a widespread cultural trend, and there should be little wonder that their comments conform with and articulate the emerging principles of the era at hand.

Common to all three is a new way of looking—a mode of perception which strips the object of previously endowed meanings and makes it clear that significance is a quality not of the thing itself but of the human activity taking place around it. Barthes notes this process at work in the nouveau roman, and Hassan senses it in the play of signification favored by innovative fictionists in America, but the initial formulation is made by Rosenberg, who transforms the entire way we see paintings by giving a new prominence to act. "Action Painting is a realistic movement," he insists, "though in it there are no pictures of things. It is the reality of the artist at the moment that he is painting. This is the most concentrated reality one can think of" (*CBR*, p. 207). Rosenberg's notion of Action Painting as it elucidates the work of Pollock, de Kooning, Hofmann, and others has been debated by many critics and painters, including Irving Sandler and Lee Krasner, but the point is not just its pertinence to the artwork at hand but its contribution to the habit of postmodern thought, a style which eclipses particular artists and paintings. What is interesting about Rosenberg's new axiom is that its shift in emphasis from the finished work to its making—and especially the rehearsal of that making by the art audience—changes our notion of what art is. Signs, whether as paintings or elements of social behavior, are simply the result of a human activity, and such sign-*making* is more interesting than the finished sign and certainly tells us more about human creativity. The viewer should be less concerned with the artwork's objective presence than with the evidence it presents of the artist's action, which is the true signature of a work. It is this same sense of activity that draws Barthes's interest in literature, which *stages* language instead of just using it to represent a thought. As a semiologist, Barthes can investigate the languages of social custom to show how they and not their objects create desire; key examples are fashion advertising and sports reporting, but the practice applies to any grammar of signs. It is not the cape or sweater or the presence of a Tour de France bicycle racer which signifies; it is the fashion or sports system's assertion which does, just as the painter's activity with paint (not the representation on the canvas) conveys meaning.

Rosenberg, Barthes, and Hassan are interested not in the historical origin of artworks or even in a structural analysis of their form, but rather in deconstructing the work so that creative activity can be seen. For all three the cultural object is considered a production, with representation yielding to action, signification stepping aside for an interest in *signifiance* (Barthes's coinage for the radiant, explosive play of meanings within a text, as opposed to the strict identity of the sign with the thing signified), and the logical causality of human existence disappearing in favor of a new pervasiveness of unfettered mind. What occurs in the consideration of a product—reference, meaning, order, authority, and the like—becomes less important than the mobile action of signifiers implied by production, which is now much more revealing than the ultimate signified.

Such a shift creates a new role for the reader or art audience, as what is confronted in a novel or painting is not a form to be admired but rather the problematic action of an individual at work with his or her materials, the nature of which remains in evidence to be considered along with the final effect. Instead of an illusory sense of representation, the reader/viewer is now treated to an action which can happen in his or her life—to be viewed not as images of nature or civilization represented by words or paint but rather as the evidence of words or paint worked with by the writer/artist. Such works do not *mean* but rather *confront*, creating a sense of action as dramatic as that of their composition. Indeed, the most successful postmodern novels and paintings keep the actions of making and viewing as close as possible, as the work is always happening when read or seen. Meanings are plural rather than singular, contributing to the sense that the ultimate act of writing or painting is completed by the audience—the measure of success is not the work's finality but rather the amount of production it brings to the reader/viewer. To read is to discover how a text was written; to view a painting is to see how it was painted. One places oneself within the production, not the product, and for this to happen the audience must free itself of all inhibitions and presumptions of meaning. By doing so language, line, and gesture are restored to their active energy, making the work a true realm of productivity where maker and audience meet.

Movement is the key element in the aesthetics of postmodern thought. Such activity, especially on the part of the reader/viewer, physically enlarges the novel or painting and provides an enhanced appreciation. Arising out of movement, the work is received as movement, and for once the essence of art can be located in an identity of production and reception. As long as contact with this process is maintained, the artwork continues to exist; on the other hand, a sense of contact prevents extraneous elements from interfering and diverting the imaginative act—in this way postmodernism prevents political misreadings motivated by materials outside the textual or painterly activity. The movement within the artwork is just that, a structure of activity which by its interrelationship assumes a double sense of artifice. The structure of a work is its only content, but that structure positively contains the work to the extent that it is not the constituent element but its place which matters. Again the postmodern aesthetic asserts itself, urging that the truth of a work lies not in its depth but in its extent. Here is the field of action for the maker, who invests the truth of a work, not in its messages or psychological expressivity, but in the evidence of his or her hand pressing down to create a trace in paint or language. Inside no longer commands outside; there is no kernel of meaning to be cracked, only a texture of activity to be experienced in its making. The surface and extent of the artwork are the places where creativity are to be found.

To clarify such an aesthetic Rosenberg embarks upon his de-definition of art, Barthes conducts his deconstruction of semiotic systems, and Hassan uncovers the presumptive constraints lurking behind humanistic thought. These processes involve a certain amount of anti-art, anti-literature, and anti-metaphysics in order to strip away qualities which readers and viewers have previously thought necessary to form an artwork, but Rosenberg, Barthes, and Hassan are ultimately interested in a more positive view. The result is to reemphasize the shift from product to maker and from artwork to performer. The writer/artist starts with an action and notes what happens; criticism reconstructs this process, just as the semiologist uncovers the action of sign systems in their making. The materials of this process are not sacrificed in the critical vision to an understanding of purpose. Instead, they are seen as an absolute substance whose glory is manifested in their human use. Hence the perfect wedding of substance and structure, which Barthes relates to the founding of structuralist thought in Saussure's metaphor of linguistics—the famous 8:25 p.m. Geneva-Paris express, which despite its necessary daily variation of locomotive, cars, and crew remains the same train, precisely because the human activity of its making deems it so.

These are the qualities of thought which bespeak the postmodern style of our times. Of the sense of modernism that remains, what is most remarkable is its tenacity. "When will the Modern period end?" Ihab Hassan asks with some exasperation. "Has ever a period waited so long? Renaissance? Baroque? Neo-Classic? Romantic? Victorian? Perhaps only the Dark Middle Ages" (*P*, p. 40). Harold Rosenberg begins his first book with a similar complaint, removed from later editions after modernism's power had faded, about the lingering sense of crisis and regret which inhibited an understanding of mankind's new cultural inheritance. Modernism in decline could yield only nihilism, historical despair, and a distrust of the psyche (once psychoanalyzed) that abandoned the self to a meaningless if not aggressively hostile universe. Against the postmodern promise of endless creative play (thanks to the understanding of life as action and reality as a system for those acts), modernism sings a tuneless song of exhaustion—witness the-death-of-the-novel controversy which centers on the depletion of conventional techniques rather than on the invention of new ones. Modernism's only positive contribution, as Roland Barthes shows, is a fraudulent attempt to find the universal in every situation, even when this entails willfully confusing the eternal with the temporal and ignoring the particular nature of materials and events.

This need for grounding artworks in the universal characterizes modernism's taste for authority, a disposition which makes it hard to leave the scene gracefully, especially in favor of a habit of thought which privileges chance over necessity and randomness over preconceived order. When Rosenberg compares art movements, he notices a preference for the eye in modernism and for the hand in what comes after. Giving way to the hand in such circumstances means abandoning just what modernism treasures, which is meditation over improvisation and form over action. In Barthes's celebrated attempt to expose the naturalization of history into the cultural, which happens when an authoritarian economy attempts to impose its ideas as being universally ordained instead of being arbitrary conventions of artifice and event, may be found the explanation for modernism's dogged persistence: its refusal to admit that its groundings are merely institutional and not cosmically necessary. In Hassan's contrast of modernism's aristocratic sense of authority with postmodernism's preference for immanence and indeterminacy, the subversive and even anarchic sense of the new movement's posture toward its predecessor is clear.

Postmodern writers and artists, however, are not nihilists; that is a modernist assumption more pertinent to its own depleted possibilities. Instead, the motive is affirmative: by declining to represent a sign, the postmodern maker gives us the ultimate sign, which is that of his or her presence at work in the activity of creation. What is created is the artist's self, and the emphasis on action above order means the self can be remade at will. Such an action suggests that the measure of human action is enlarged beyond the previously circumscribed possibilities of meditation and form, just as Ihab Hassan sees the mind breaking out of the body's constraints and filling the universe with its presence. To those who argue such liberations were proposed within modernism by such movements as Surrealism and Dada, Harold Rosenberg quickly notes that in these projects an artificial release of concentration simply freed the mind to return to the data of nature and memory. Only the genuine spontaneity of Action Painting guarantees a new world. There is nothing to be uncovered from the realm of dream and subconscious in postmodern art—no hidden world to discover, for everything is to be made anew, based on the type of event out of which the self is formed. In postmodern writing and painting, mind becomes one with the page or canvas; no modernistic objective correlatives are needed to communicate between maker and viewer.

In the second edition of his *Dismemberment of Orpheus* (pp. 267–68), Ihab Hassan outlines the radical contrasts between the two eras. Instead of seeking purpose as did the moderns, postmodernists revel in play; the hierarchal principles by which modernism carefully structured a sense of order are replaced by the unpredictable, favoring the randomness of a work in progress over its static, finished state. There is no sense of totalized meaning in postmodernism; quite the contrary, semiologists deconstruct such presumptions to reveal the arbitrariness of constraints. The sense of illusion necessary for metaphor's identification of one entity with another yields to the more integral process of metonymy in which each element can remain itself. Surface replaces depth as the location of an artwork's essence, because surface is where the art-making activity takes place and is reenacted by the audience. Modernism's hallowed forms of meaning, determinacy and transcendence, are now faulted for misdirecting attention from the artwork itself; postmodernism's respect for materials and the artist/writer's action on and within them privileges the immanence of the painting or text itself. Most significantly for an emerging habit of thought, the maker's goal is no longer seen as the signification of some other reality but is rather accepted as its own process in action; once paint is seen as its own substance and language is received, not as a transparent window, but as an opaque system of differences whose only true reference is to itself, then the artwork can be appreciated, not as the correspondence with an ideal order, but rather a display of the maker's compositional sense of how the game of life is played.

If there is a common key to this postmodern habit of thought, it is the lesson learned from language: that the authentic phenomenon in any event is not *fact*, but *relationship*. Here may be found the principle for Rosenberg's Action Painting, Barthes's semiology of naturalization, and Hassan's interpenetration of culture and mind. Labels such as *postmodernism* are a culture's relentless struggle to understand itself, "presuming its uniqueness in history" as Hassan suggests in *The Postmodern Turn* (p. xi), and the special attribute common to the time Rosenberg, Barthes, and Hassan share is the understanding not just that the central values of a culture are expressed in its myths but that those myths are, as Hassan reminds us, formed like a language—and that "language destabilizes, even topples, any claim to transcendent 'truth'" (*GS*, p. 331). Barthes adds that language, "by its 'obligatory rubrics' (and not only by its exclusions), compels us to think in a certain way" (*RL*, p. 3), and Rosenberg confirms that "Art in its old form—an objective classification of objects—has come to an end, swallowed up in a sea of image-making without boundaries" (*ASM*, p. 6).

Authority is undermined, canons fall; no one thing can be more "artistic" or "literary" than any other when it comes to a priori criteria, for the test is in the act, not in the anticipation or the institutionalized aftermath. The work is "destabilized," "unmargined," in Ihab Hassan's words (*MS*, p. 448; *PMT*, p. 201); and so with theory unseated, performance gains new eminence and action preempts idea. "It is not the occupant of meaning which determines the work," Barthes advises, "it is his *place*" (*RL*, p. 174); and the being of literature is within its making, within the act of writing; any language unaware of its own existence acts in bad faith. Now, instead of the totalitarian ideology of the referent we can glory in the act of production, an exercise Hassan relates to the stage in human development when dream, language, and imagination make their presence felt and "the brain [begins] to bully the genes in the story of evolution" (*MS*, p. 438; *PMT*, p. 192). Learning expands the human environment—a lesson from Piaget; with "Providence" out of the way, sense becomes something to be made and discovered. Language itself is substituted for the subject "hitherto supposed to be its owner," as Barthes explains (*RL*, p. 50); the text or artwork is no longer a sacred object but a space of language, whether that language be the grammar of signs or of an artist's consecutive acts—the creator is born simultaneously with his or her work. This work is a braid of several codes, the workings of which "rustle" as their presence is felt, "the noise of what is working well" (*RL*, p. 76); attention is shifted from the functional notations of use to the painting's or text's "work, to its delight [*jouissance*]: how the word 'rummages' in the inter-text" (*RL*, p. 249).

This new activity places fresh emphasis on the reader and viewer. Instead of the channeling of author-dominated work, postmodern art and writing disperse their force among their audience, "the site where structure is made hysterical" (*RL,* p. 43). The space of such work is to be traversed for the experience, not pierced to reveal some hidden meaning, for the unity of a work is not in its origin but in its destination, with reality being the shared experience of "the reality of the artist at the moment as he is painting" (*CBR,* p. 207), the structure by which Harold Rosenberg brings action into infinite play.

Because the opposite of this postmodern tendency is the role of myth, which turns culture into nature (and hence transports it to the realm of static unquestionability), Hassan is especially concerned to find a philosophy appropriate to our time. His choice is that most American of philosophies, Pragmatism, which fits the postmodern habit of thought because it "brackets Truth (capitalized), circumvents Metaphysics and Epistemology," and "finds no universal 'ground' for discourse" (*MS,* p. 451; *PMT,* p. 204). It is a wise choice because Pragmatism shares postmodern uncertainty without abdicating judgment, and in the case of William James adopts a mood that is as expansive and celebratory as Rosenberg's Action Painting and Barthes's dance of signs at play. Pragmatism supplies the praxis which is the counterpart of painting's action and language's play; it is "a transactive model, one that keeps traditional distinctions in abeyance, that sublates or transumes or even forgets them *provisionally*" (*PMT,* p. 227). Critics of postmodernism have decried its lack of authority and center, but Hassan's plan supplies a "new fideology, less a science than pragmatics or maieutics of belief" (*PMT,* p. xv). The central issue of our time, after all, is "of meaning, of *belief*" (*GS,* p. 320), and a Jamesian sense of provisional expansion allows such action without compromising what we know about the relative state of existence.

For Hassan, the expanding self generates a story of quest, "our alliance with risk [transposed] into a sustained vision" (*Q,* p. 125). Here is the vital present "in which we do not stand apart from life, we *are* life" (*Q,* p. 137). The posture recalls Roland Barthes's from the last years of his life, when the loss of his own life-long center (his mother) prompted him to try a novel, for "its power is the truth of affects, not of ideas" (*RL,* p. 289). This loving power of the novel—of the imagination *in action*—is perhaps the final, yet-to-be-achieved development of postmodern thought, at which point it would become the artistic act itself. To align one's role with Art, not with Priesthood—this may be the last ambition of the postmodern thinker. From Rosenberg through Barthes to Hassan, one sees the thinker getting closer to this goal.

Together, these three thinkers reflect a major transposition in how the artistic imagination functions and is received. Each argues for a fundamental change in the nature of the medium, as Rosenberg removes the act of art from representative depth to the surface of applied action, as Barthes transforms the act of writing from a reflective medium into a basically intransitive act whose reference is primarily to itself, and as Hassan reenvisions the place of mankind in the material and spiritual universe. In their seminal statements can be found a refrain—"at a certain moment," "at what point," "coming to an end"—which sounds the epochal chord in their symphony of mind and aesthetics. All three sense that a major period in art and thought has come to an end. But in this change they sense new possibilities for human expression, and so set about the business of devising a new manner of thought.

Two

Harold Rosenberg

Art as Act

At a certain moment the canvas began to appear to one American painter after another as an arena in which to act—rather than as a space in which to reproduce, re-design, analyze or 'express' an object, actual or imagined. What was to go on the canvas was not a picture but an event. With this formulation Harold Rosenberg restructures the notion of painting for postmodernism. As the central theme of his first critical book, *The Tradition of the New* (p. 25), it presents far-reaching implications. "Whoever undertakes to create," Rosenberg cautions, "soon finds himself engaged in creating himself" (*TN*, p. 10), and so human nature itself and not just the artistic act is re-visioned.

That Rosenberg's thesis helps inaugurate a new aesthetic is apparent from the combative sense with which he sees it opposed to the lingering cultural sense of modernism. The book's title has announced his larger historical thesis, that "The famous 'modern break with tradition' has lasted long enough to have produced its own tradition" (*TN*, p. 9), but in two paragraphs removed from later editions (when the postmodern spirit had gained more popular acceptance) he explains how this new practice of ongoing innovation met with resistance in the 1950s:

> At present this recognition is stubbornly refused. The living tradition of our time, half-buried from the start, is driven farther underground by a traditionalist propaganda exploiting a widespread mood of crisis and regret. The notion of the "disinheritance of modern man" has become the most influential platitude in the intellectual world today. Everything from birth control to safe-driving courses in high school—to say nothing of totalitarian brutalities and the "faceless mobs" of megapolis—is interpreted as a symptom of lost blood-heritage. The characteristic features of the century are regarded as a mask for the void.
>
> Under the rule of this fixed idea, nothing can be understood. Mystification combined with moral outrage (or moral surrender) attends each fresh move in art, each new coalescence in politics. The caste of intellectuals plagued by a succession of phantasies regarding the past turns into a cast of professional mystifiers. (*TN*, pp. 10–11)

That Rosenberg could drop this statement from his book's second edition (1966, Collier/Macmillan) and that it need not be reinstated in the collected edition of his works (published by the University of Chicago Press in 1983) indicates how radically cultural conditions had changed during the intervening years, an argument borne out by political and social analyses as well. But most important is the fact that his new view of artistic creation was posited directly against an exhausted notion of modernism itself. The absurdist product would now be replaced by an essentially subjectless art, a celebration of process which would be sufficient as its own event. When the break with tradition is formalized as a major axiom in a new tradition itself, the adjective "post" becomes an apt revision of modernism.

Favoring the modern in postmodern times is akin to ignoring the American present and following outmoded European standards instead. Rosenberg considers this to be an "hallucination of displaced terrain" and calls it "Redcoatism" (*TN*, p. 14). Extending this Revolutionary War metaphor, he finds the opposite practice to be "Coonskinism," which in terms of aesthetics is "the search for the principle that applies, even if it applies only once" (*TN*, p. 19). Appreciative that each situation may have its own key, the postmodern temper reveals itself in post–World War II American art which accepts the "creative bearings of such elements of creation as the mistake, the accident, the spontaneous, the incomplete, the absent" (*TN*, p. 21). Yet central to Rosenberg's posture as a critic is this sense of opposition to the modern, a development out of and away from the European—for this is what, in his first full-length study of an artist, *Arshile Gorky,* Rosenberg hails as "the *romance* of post-War American painting" (p. 13).

This celebratory sense of the new pervades Rosenberg's work, from the opening lines of *Discovering the Present,* which announce the demise of modernism, to the thesis of his study *Barnett Newman,* which argues that Western Art's "exaltation of the aesthetic" had "step by step deprived itself of the power to deal with man's deepest experiences" (p. 29). The moral shocks of our century were forcing art to turn beyond its European tradition, and in a new style of American action Rosenberg found the perfect means of expression. Action is a consistent principle throughout his critical work, and often its formulation is repeated verbatim: "The innovation of Action Painting was to dispense with the representation of the state in favor of enacting it in the physical movement of painting. The action on the canvas became its own representation" (*AO*, p. 158; *TN*, p. 27). Action is by nature sign-producing, he points out, leaving the trace of a movement whose origin is never fully revealed. *Sign* and *trace* are, of course, the language of Barthes and Derrida, and Rosenberg's vocabulary is not coincidental to their purpose. His ultimate interest is the sign of passage of the artist's body, just as Barthes and Derrida follow the motions of man the sign-making animal as he constructs the systems by which he conducts his life (as if in a naturalized manner). Each process testifies to the creation at hand, leaving behind the created object simply as an indicator of how it has been produced.

For this to happen, the art object must be extinguished in favor of the act. Rosenberg appreciates the work of Pollock, de Kooning, and the other Action painters because their business with the canvas has been organized with the emotional and intellectual energy of a living situation. It is not "self-expression," for that implies "the acceptance of the ego as it is, with its wound and its magic" (*TN*, p. 28). Instead the canvas gives us the ego in action, responding not to itself but to its participation in the world. There are modernist anticipations of this practice, which in a 1967 essay Rosenberg traces to the time "the Cubists began shifting positions before the model and composing out of 'angle shots' " (*ASM*, p. 11). But it is when energy itself is projected that Action Painting takes place and a key to the postmodern aesthetic is born; instead of depicting action (as modernists, and most certainly the Futurists had done), the point was now to be itself the artist's action, just as the artwork, from Dada and Surrealism through the Happening, had been acquiring the status of an event. Vanguard movements as a whole had sought "to liquidate art as a classification of objects and to re-define it in terms of the intellectual acts of artists" (*AO*, p. 17), but when the "act-painting is of the same metaphysical substance as the artist's existence," the "new painting has broken down every distinction between art and life" (*TN*, p. 28).

Like Barthes and Derrida, Rosenberg is quick to avoid any sense of a rarified aesthetic by relating it directly to practical concerns. "Can one doubt that it was the challenge to action on the streets that was to lead in the next decade to the response in practice that took place on the canvas?" he asks in *Arshile Gorky*. "To the pragmatic ideologies of the Depression the pragmatic response of art was to be Action Painting," specifically because post-Cubist abstraction could not "meet the needs of painting in America" (*AG*, pp. 93–94). The rationale of both art and social history, as evidenced by the fate of Thirties' radicalism, was bankrupt, and hence the artist turns to direct engagement so that his or her painting is "a record of the art activity to which its creator has surrendered" (*AG*, p. 102). Rather than solving artistic problems, which might indeed be considered as abstract from life, the artist "lives it through the instrumentality of his materials" (*AO*, p. 19), an example of directly applied pragmatism. The artist is simply the first spectator to this process; the audience is invited to share the experience of having the work take shape, and thus itself thinks in "a vocabulary of action: its inception, duration, direction—psychic state, concentration and relaxation of the will, passivity, alert waiting" (*TN*, p. 29). In terms of an absolute practicality for art, what could be more immediate and more democratic?

The artwork, then, is identical with the processes which have created it, and in this sense it continues in existence. Jackson Pollock saw the painting as an instance of contact—as long as the contact was maintained, the artwork continued to happen, and this process of remaining in touch with the work is sustained by its audience. Willem de Kooning expands the sense of contact by taking risks, "gambling with the possible destruction of each work-in-progress by holding it open to associations that spring up in the course of its association" (*WDK*, p. 35). Automatism, that remnant of modernist indulgence which an unfriendly culture might receive as one more element of absurdity, was for Pollock just a means "to unlock the activity of painting and release it from dependence upon concepts" (*AP*, p. 62). Once engaged, the artist would certainly be aware of this action, particularly since its progress is often a lengthy business consisting of all the choices, hesitations, and accidents he or she privileges the viewer to reenact. Pollock's consciousness is thus concerned not at all with an effect "determined by notions of good painting" but rather "toward the protraction and intensification of the doing itself, of the current that flows between the artist and his marked-out world and whose pauses, drifts, detours, and tides lift him into 'pure harmony'" (*AP*, p. 62).

The notion of the art object as its own activity is the most frequently cited principle in Rosenberg's work, and the range of occasions on which he employs it indicates its breadth in his aesthetic. It includes Suzanne Langer's central idea of the "art symbol," in which the oeuvre "stands apart" from the artist, not as a sign pointing to the artist's feelings but as "a creation, an appearance or 'semblance,' in which the thought, passion and craft of the creator take on a transformed life" (*TN*, p. 52). For Arshile Gorky, the abstract artwork is an occasion for "making experience over through a protracted series of connected efforts" to the point that it becomes "a 'mind' through which the artist discovers, by means of manual and mental hypotheses, signs of what he is or might be" (*AG*, p. 118). In the sculptures of Barnett Newman, Rosenberg sees something beyond the nonobjective and nonrepresentational, "an art that brought a new reality into being, the reality of the idea" (*BNS*, p. 11). Looking at a de Kooning canvas, the critic finds a new sense of integrity based on the materials and motions of art themselves, to the point that "each gesture of the brush that goes into its composition is a totality in itself" (*AP*, p. 217). Art derives from life, and in some cases becomes identical with it, but "neither the artist nor the painting has a character that pre-exists their encounter" (*AO*, p. 111), and it is within this sense of encounter that Action Painting exists. For Barnett Newman, that encounter yields a silent presence (especially in his paintings); with Pollock and de Kooning, the canvas has more shimmer and dance, but these works too are added to the world to be encountered like a rock or a refrigerator, as things most evidently *there*—"a performance, which like an event in history is enlarged in retrospect" (*AO*, p. 123). Performances are indeed real; consider a battle, or crossing an ocean. These are the metaphors, epic in nature, which occur to Rosenberg when he discusses de Kooning at work. Barnett Newman parallels this act when his vertical line divides the canvas into two rectangles—no figure is represented, yet the canvas "becomes an 'object,' like a votive monument in a sacrificial grove" (*DDA*, p. 96).

Turning from artist to work, we see that as a corollary of action, materials tend to influence effect. Size itself becomes a material consideration, contributing to the work's blatant presence. To be "in" his paintings, Jackson Pollock took them off the wall or easel and tacked them to the floor, and poured paint rather than letting a brush intercede. "Contentless agitations of materials" (*AP*, p. 67) is how Rosenberg describes some of the resultant canvases, although Barnett Newman achieved the same sense of monumental presence by conceiving painting in terms of its fundamental elements and then working to destroy each element "by derailing it from its accepted uses in art of the past" (*BN*, p. 56), which in turn brought new attention to its materiality.

A second corollary of Action Painting is that the artist becomes more conscious of other artworks; his or her working universe of reference is no longer the natural world, but rather art history. As far as material beyond the act of painting itself, Action Painting turns increasingly to the experience of other art, leading to an increased density of meaning. There are references even within an artist's oeuvre, such as the *Woman*-ish pinks which turn up in de Kooning's later landscapes. Arshile Gorky's work is distinguished by the painter's ability to return to allusion, yet at each step discard a bit of depiction without ever losing meaning; to the extent that colors, shapes, and movements could evoke emotional states, Gorky was able to embrace abstract art. At times, a rejection of outright originality can be the most original act. But still the avant garde performs the crucial task of de-definition, for "Only the pressure of new creations *against* art as it has been defined keeps art from merging with the media and allows work to survive for an interval as art" (*ASM*, p. 51). Hence the validity for styles originating within abstract ideas and idea-based art movements, and for the success of works whose effect has been to discredit and even destroy styles which have turned into clichés—witness Frank Stella's career which has thrived on an aptitude for debate with the visual techniques of others. The very uncertainty of what constitutes art thus encourages a vitality of production.

But Rosenberg's sense of deconstruction is foremost a part of art becoming action rather than representation. This motive has led to the de-definition Rosenberg finds in the step-by-step subtraction of traditional attributes by which paintings have been known, from pictorial subject, line, and color to even the work's suspension on the wall—not as a Dadaistic spectacle in itself, but so that the activity of process might be given more room for exercise. As always, the emphasis is on new creation:

> The *modern* modern [postmodern] poet or painter, as distinguished from the old modern artist, picks his way among the bits and pieces of the cultural heritage and puts together whatever seems capable of carrying a meaning. The Action painter does this putting together in an original and lively way. He starts an action and observes what kind of image it will magnetize out of the formal accretions piled up in his mind. He is a kind of archeologist, one who digs in himself, not just among modern art movements. (*AP*, p. 216)

Hence the shift in critical emphasis from product to performer, in which the work derives its meaning from the principle personified by its creator. In these circumstances the proper matter for criticism becomes the total activity by which the artist structures his or her life, subject only to the art forms provided by their era of culture.

Technology's impact on the modern age had occasioned a despair that truly creative art was no longer possible, but Rosenberg's post-

Jackson Pollock,
"Greyed Rainbow,"
1953. Gift of the Society
for Contemporary
American Art. © 1987
The Art Institute of Chi-
cago. All Rights
Reserved.

21
Harold
Rosenberg:
Art as
Act

modern conception of what the artist does resolves this problem. "Art is one of the few things left that a human being can do in which he can completely control the material he uses, whether it's an idea or physical matter," he told a conference on art and technology:

> The function of art to me is very clear. It's the one opportunity that human beings have within our society to make something themselves and in that way make their own selves. In industry a type is invented and then people are made to conform to the type. People become artists in our society in order to escape being made into something else. (*CBR*, p. 77)

Turning back from the artwork to its maker, one sees the greatest implication of Rosenberg's aesthetic: that by the principles of Action Painting, the self is remade at will. This is why the study of art is no longer the classification of objects, but rather a comprehension of the painter's intellectual and physical act. Apart from their execution, these works have no secure identity—hence their status as what Rosenberg calls "anxious objects" (*AO*, p. 17) which must declare themselves as art rather than exist passively. For the artist, there is no world to discover, for everything is to be made anew, and made of nothing except the painter's activity with materials. As a result, there is a fresh emphasis on making, and in these practices the undertaking of art finds a discipline for the shaping of an individuality. Focusing on the psychic experience of creation brings the artist closer to his or her materials, and also (through a kinship with other artists, past and present) to a sense of art as celebration and magic. There is a pronounced metaphysical dimension to this remaking of the self through art-action. A typical Giacometti sculpture, thanks to its evocation of rituals and talismans, transforms the human body into a spiritual substance as the artist uses fable to theatricalize contemporary fact. Reality is personal, "a flash struck from dead space by an ecstatic apprehension of particulars" (*AE*, p. 125), and the evidence of this flash is in the making of the sculpture and in its declared presence as act. Metaphysical longings bring the postmodern artist face to face with nothingness, but unlike the modernist response of representing this sense of void with the signs and practices of previous cultures, Rosenberg's painters and sculptors attain the absolute without resorting to inherited beliefs. As in the work of Barnett Newman, the presence of his act is all the spiritual reality that is needed.

By confronting in daily practice the problematic nature of postmodern individuality, Action Painting returns art to its metaphysical purpose. Yet this time around, illusion is not necessary, for the style of art Rosenberg champions draws the spectator into a realm which, although it is invented in the painter's gesture, is in substance identical to the actions of the viewer's life—only now that action is celebrated in the act of art, both its making and its viewing. Rather than representing landscapes, for example, the canvas itself becomes a domain (as valid as any geography) which is taken into the world of art by the painter's act and the spectator's view of it. It is the presence of the artist and the viewer that makes it a work of art. There is a sense of mystery to individual identity, but postmodern art invents this self so that it may paint the picture—witness the drawings of Saul Steinberg in which this notion becomes a theme. The purpose here is not just the production of an art object, but a continuum of events of which the artwork remains as evidence; every piece is in fact a piece of the artist who made it, and its meaning derives from the spectator's appreciation of this totality. When the painter's imagination can no longer conceive of pictures of what happens, then the idea itself must be painted, as with Barnett Newman's canvases. Dimensions of the individual are alternately expanded and contracted, with the emphasis on the act itself. For a painter such as Pollock, de Kooning, or Hofmann, "What he seeks is not a sign representing a hidden self, the unconscious, but *an event* out of which a self is formed, as it is formed out of other kinds of action when those actions are free and sufficiently protracted" (*AP*, p. 226, italics added). There is no world, only a world to make, as the artist originates something that has never been seen before. As Rosenberg concludes, "Nature begins in the artist" (*AO*, p. 84).

The world unfolds from the artist's act: Saul Steinberg's drawings thematize this notion, just as a Pollock canvas is essentially an inscription of his identity. A choice in execution affects that identity, as de Kooning's improvisations risk each work he is completing. But as a result art becomes more closely engaged with the organic life of its maker. The most characteristic human action is to make a form, and as unbidden forms spring up reality is created anew. That such a change in cultural sensibility is at hand becomes clear in Rosenberg's review of Marshall McLuhan's *Understanding Media,* where he notes that "For the first time in history, the media are providing us with extensions not of one or more sense organs but of our sense structure as a whole" (*CBR,* p. 62). As the artist exists within the execution of his or her painting, so humankind exists in its language—exists holistically, beyond the split personality which resulted from the desensualization of print media. In his collection of social essays, *Act and the Actor,* Rosenberg explores this belief that no matter what contemporary event he was studying, everything returned to the notion of the actor forming his identity through acts. Hence, as with Barnett Newman's sculptures, shape alone can form the act of creation, apart from other elements, since it is the act of Newman's thinking, directed as it is toward ecstasy, which transcends the need for anything else—the wholeness of his vision is present in the chosen shape.

Turning to the physical state of the artwork itself, Rosenberg argues that traditional elements are not so much negated as reinvented. Hans Hofmann, for example, used a model for his classes which produced abstract expressionist work: with attention directed to the model, students were taught to appreciate not the isolated figure but the energies and forces whose conflux gave shape to the space she occupied. Depicting this larger sense of presence thus transcended the conventions of realism. Hofmann's classroom practice of *learning to see* thus calls for plastic creation on the canvas's flat surface without destroying this surface as a locus of energy, and the result is a dynamism of the picture which takes precedence over the truth of the scene—his famous effect of push and pull. But again, this exploitation of the surface offers more and not less than traditional art. Renaissance perspective, Hofmann taught, took the picture surface and made it the equivalent of a hole in the wall, its perspective reaching in just one direction of depth. Such space is sterile, not pictorial, and Hofmann's innovation was to make the entire picture surface answer to the touch of his brush. Depiction, in terms of pictorial creation, is therefore a much more active mode than before. Hofmann's push and pull is dynamic, but the understated effect of Barnett Newman's "zips" across the canvas yields the added dimension of the evenly surfaced emblematic composition enhanced by agitated, improvisational play, a virtual combination of what Rosenberg called "the two emerging wings of Abstract Expressionism" (*BN,*

p. 52), Rothko-Gottlieb-Reinhardt and Pollock-de Kooning-Hofmann. Here too Rosenberg's notion of the act comes into play, as "The notion of a *field* of action is an interesting alternative to the traditional idea of a plot as a *structure* of actions" (*AA*, p. 106). He looks back to Dostoevsky's *The Idiot* to find an analogy of a work spreading outward to envelop as many aspects as possible, instead of remaining with the simple continuity of linear progression—just as Hofmann's exploitation of the surface multiplies the dimensions of perspective.

Focus is another element enlarged rather than discarded by Action Painting. A typical canvas by Barnett Newman allows the eye to rove in undistracted motion within the work's pigmentation, and when this action is a part of the work's presence the result is more and not less, as the work arises out of movement, takes form within it (as if congealed), and is perceived as movement by the viewer. Space is enlarged, and with it the artist's opportunities. By themselves, Barnett Newman's shapes imply the infinities of space and succeed without other elements; on the other hand, his shapes can be quite definite, assuming the presence of objects and standing concretely in space, just as space itself is created around his sculptures. Like the canvas before it is painted, space is the essential absence every artist confronts. Rosenberg's aesthetic allows this element to become more productive. A truly complex element, space is the "nothing wrapped around every object in the world, soothing or strangling it" (*DP*, p. 72), and when the postmodern artist employs it in his or her work, the dimensions of both the artistic act and the work produced are increased.

Using space relates more to the conditions of painting than to painting itself, but as with Hofmann's expanded dimensions of perspective it invites a new vision of art as a practice by which the artist is transformed:

> That Newman's rectangles are real and living shapes means that they cannot be produced by external calculation but that the artist must enter into them as spatial indeterminacies which he brings to certain dimensions in the experience of painting them, as one holds or even cuts short an interval of breath. (*AO*, p. 173)

In his *Woman* series, Willem de Kooning adopts the same style of practice, perceiving the woman neither as the static image posed in the composition nor as one of the many colored shapes perceived by the artist. Instead, "she and her environment are apprehended simultaneously as a complex of evanescent sensations, passions, and transient moods—and this soluble amalgam can be recalled to life only in the act of painting" (*WDK*, p. 33), elaborating on the lesson taught in Hans Hofmann's life class. The canvas captures this interplay of actions between figure and field, yielding the record of a visual encounter which is always ready to be replayed by the viewer—something which in its activity transforms the viewer as a factor in this new reality. De Kooning looks past the painting as object to its event, to its mode of creation, and in doing so frees himself from the coercion of art history as a purely evolutionary process. But neither is art history discarded, for by focusing on its principle of creation a work can be reinvented infinitely.

Yet in the final analysis, depiction—whether of object or event—is a response to nature, and therefore it is important to see how Rosenberg's postmodernism shares a key principle with Michel Foucault, who demonstrated that what Western society considers as "Nature" is simply the system of constraints by which such norms are established, and with Roland Barthes, whose studies showed how arbitrary signs are "naturalized" by long usage into a bourgeois standard of order. As Rosenberg writes in his text for Saul Steinberg's *Le Masque* (Paris: Maeght Editeur, 1966):

> Ce que nous appelons "nature" est, en réalité, la somme des styles qui coexistent en une période donnée: la nature est ornementale, "Naturaliste," abstraite, primitive. . . . Cette vieille banalité que "la nature imite l'art" s'est vue investir, au Vingtième siècle, d'une puissance supérieure, par la surimpression toute physique dont ont marqué la terre et ses créatures les inventions humaines. (p. 18)

> What we call nature is, in reality, the sum of styles which coexist in a given period: nature is decorative, "Naturalistic," abstract, primitive. . . . This old banality that "nature imitates art" was invested, in the twentieth century, with a superior power by the physical superimposition which had labeled the earth and its creatures as human inventions.

Therefore Steinberg draws only things which have been made over by mankind, for it is this transformation which makes them interesting.

Depiction becomes less a matter of recording than of commenting, as he captures the imprints of society rather than society itself. Here is depiction without representation, no less than Barnett Newman or Mark Rothko strove for in their own work. Rothko's major achievement was determining and measuring what was irreducible in art; by refusing to represent a sign, the painter arrives at an ultimate sign, the sign of mankind's spiritual presence. For Steinberg the result can be whimsical, for Rothko profound, but the motive is much the same, together with the aesthetic by which it is produced. Steinberg's quasi-representations in fact draw themselves, just as Rothko's sense of volume, tone, and especially color create his paintings before us. This play of color, formed in oblongs, determines the work's emotional content, to the point that not just representation but materiality itself is overcome, just as the material sense of Steinberg's world yields to the act of its depiction, one more example of art as event. That this aesthetic is capable of progression and development is seen in the apparently opposite tendencies of Pop Art, where in fact the artist depicts not real things but pictures of things, and where the inherent detachment from content allows everything, from a Turner sunset to a Shell Oil sign, to be treated equally. There is even a transcendence of representation in Tinguely's self-destructive "Homage to New York," which is "not only the most recent of the elected aesthetic representatives of the century but the most perfect: it has succeeded in not existing" (*DDA*, p. 156). But Rosenberg's most serious and most convincing example is Barnett Newman, whose works achieved the reality of feeling without figurative content.

Locating this postmodern aesthetic within the actual studio practices of art, rather than in the art history/university program mode of intellectualization which he so despised, is one of Rosenberg's major achievements as a critic. Action, performance, gesture, and the transformation of both artist and viewer might be consigned to the realm of the immaterial were it not for the critic's thoughtful investigations and patient explanations of what actually happens on the painting's surface. Hofmann's studio classes, Rosenberg finds, are directed toward "learning how to organize forms behind one another on the single plane of the picture surface rather than causing them to recede through the illusionary devices of perspective" (*AO*, p. 147). The student painter begins with a model, but as soon as possible the canvas takes over, for it is the essential realm of creation. Speed is encouraged as an obstacle to meditation and intellectualization; the artist's hand is to be guided not by considerations or preconceptions, but rather by "the debate of pictorial knowledge with itself" (*AO*, p. 157) as it happens on the ultimate reality of the canvas surface. When surface is given precedence, art must be something more than the Surrealists painting their dreams; it must be a place where the materials paint theirs. Privileging the materials is one of Barnett Newman's peculiar successes, for "He emptied the picture surface not by leaving it blank, but by means of paint" (*BNS*, p. 12), working with emptiness "as if it were a substance. He measured it, divided it, shaped it, colored it" (*DDA*, p. 91).

As part of his famous redefinition of the canvas as an arena in which to act, Rosenberg stresses this sense of materiality. The encounter is no longer anticipated with an image in mind; instead, with material in hand, the painter approaches another piece of material, the canvas, and the resulting image is the product of this encounter, not something that precedes it. The result might well be a surprise, because the process yields not a preconceived idea but rather something new emerging from the contact of materials within the painter's gesture—gesture alone, Rosenberg emphasizes, is not enough, and is certainly not the central point to Action Painting. Such painting puts materials in action, and it is their self-apparent play which forms the work. When size increases, it is not an enlarged version of the artist's concept, but is rather a freshly new definition, based on an activation of color and harmony of scale. Extremes of size help make the point that a painting is no longer an image but is instead a material object defined by the proportions and qualities of its worked materials. Wall or gallery space becomes the frame within which this activity may be displayed, much as a Rauschenberg combine may be measured in terms of the "yardage" its materials encompass, or a Warhol serial painting in the volume it can fill. In similar manner Larry Rivers can be seen working with indeterminate jotting, using the canvas space as a graffiti artist might take advantage of a fence or wall. Eventually action, as a painting's substance, develops into activity, and the focus of this process must be the canvas surface itself.

Surface is where the act happens, but the nature of that act is similarly a plastic affair. Rosenberg is fortunate in his gallery of artists to have not just physically active (Pollock) and religiously profound

(Newman) painters, but also someone like Saul Steinberg whose works graphically express these principles at work. A natural semiotician, Steinberg knows that "style hides the man," and that to draw from life is to study life's disguises:

> Not only the artist but everyone "becomes someone else" in becoming someone. One is thought about, thus invented. Or, as Steinberg puts it with memorable succinctness in his *Cogito* drawings: "I think, therefore Descartes is." One creates not oneself but another. Being is in the act. A drawing of women is called *Four Techniques,* as if the existence of each were someone's "how to." Another drawing carries the idea further: in *Techniques at a Party* seventeen different styles of drawing have replaced the human substance of a crowd. (SS, p. 14)

The evidence of such human invention is in style, and this is what Steinberg draws and paints. Its "power of creating assent" (AE, p. 111), a conception close if not identical to Foucault's "systems of constraint," is his ultimate subject matter, which takes shape as the forms things assume through human practice. When the artist's own use of style enhances this effect, the result is doubly impressive, such as the drawing of a couple sharing a sofa whose separation is shown by her depiction in a swirl of short pencil strokes, while he is composed in a thickly contoured mass. Energy itself can serve as content, as de Kooning and Hofmann reenact their special forms of vitality on the canvas and as Barnett Newman practices the sublime (instead of finding symbols for it).

"The innovation in Action Painting," Rosenberg states in another of his classic formulations, "was to dispense with the representation of the state in favor of enacting it in the physical movement of the painting. The action on the canvas became its own representation" (AO, p. 158). As the direct manifestation of such an act, *line* takes on increased importance, as each such line on the canvas records the actual movement of the artist's hand as a statement within the painting's aesthetics of composition. This is why strokes of color (in Hofmann), of layering and reworking (in de Kooning), and of accelerated motion itself (in Pollock) retain clear, individual identities within the picture, even as forces of conflict, instead of falling into a simple set of relationships. The paint stroke is an external thing, establishing the connection be-

Jackson Pollock, "One (Number 31, 1950)," 1950. Collection of the Museum of Modern Art, New York. Sidney and Harriet Janis Collection Fund (by exchange).

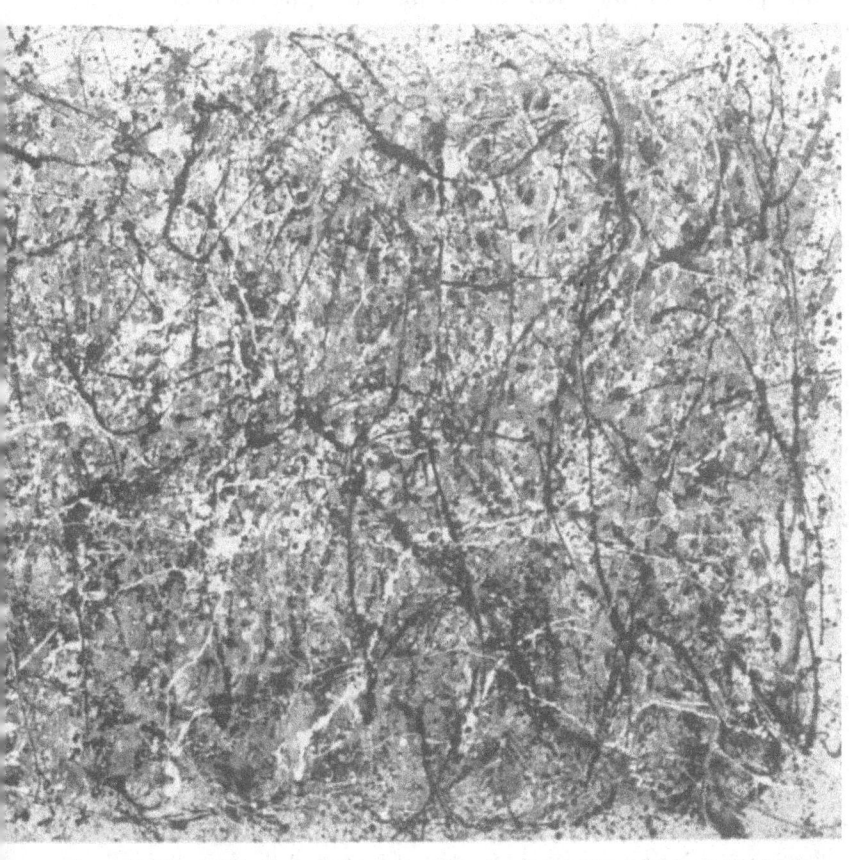

**31
Harold
Rosenberg:
Art as
Act**

tween a Kline canvas and a target-shape by Jasper Johns which by his own gesture is placed in the painting. An emphasis on line helps establish the psychological reality of the artwork, the reality of the artist at the moment he is painting, which in terms of art is certainly the most concentrated reality of all. When line itself is eclipsed, it is in the direction of the artwork deriving its meaning from whatever principle its creator personifies, but even among the first generation of Action painters the line is as characteristic as a signature—indeed, it becomes the signature itself. Signature is, after all, an evidence of the maker's presence, and the fictions which generate paintings are converted into reality through this performance, an activity of which the line on the canvas is the lingering trace.

Unlike Impressionism, Cubism, Futurism, Surrealism, or virtually any other modernist movements, Action Painting does not privilege the eye in its creation. Instead the hand determines all, from its initial investigation of volume, density, and weight in the composition to its exploratory, sometimes explosive behavior on the canvas plane. It manifests an extreme liberation from external direction, so that attention remains directed toward its action within the painting rather than on any meditated or preconceived effect. If Cubism had emphasized mind as well as eye, Action Painting did neither, often with surprising effect:

> That a meaningful image could be realized through the spontaneous "thinking" of the hand was a radical idea, if not an altogether new one—an idea which is still misunderstood by people trained to believe that all forms originate in, or are inherited by, the mind, and that consequently the absence of mental planning can only result in formlessness. The reductive (or "ascetic") symbolism developed by the contemplative Abstract Expressionists was intellectually more accessible, by association with earlier visionary painting, for example, that of Redon, than the calligraphy of the Action painters. Yet with both groups of Abstract Expressionists what counts is the tension focussed in the image by the handling—the impact of a Rothko, Newman or Gottlieb lies not in the metaphysical connotations of its oblongs, rectangles or ovals but in the expansion and compression of the surface by which the artist's psychic state is conveyed. (*AP*, pp. 125–26)

Hence the great variety within Gottlieb's canvases which will be missed entirely by the spectator not interested in his unique way of handling each work. Action Painting always invites the spectator's engagement in this creative act, and when the process works the viewer is taken up within the work rather than simply faced with it. This movement can flow both ways, and what begins with Pollock and other first generation Action painters as a regeneration of the artwork's production becomes, with Rivers, Rauschenberg, and Johns, an analysis and manipulation of the viewer's mind, employing him or her in a game, the elements of which are arranged in an appraisal of the painting. Their practice presumes a sophisticated, art-educated audience; the other side of this presumption is that anyone so educated "ceases to be a spectator and becomes in some respect a participant" (*DP*, p. 128).

The prominence of action leads to an increased emphasis on execution of line and on the handling of materials, even in the larger sense when such handling includes the viewer's reaction. But in its full expanse, the principles of postmodern art encompass the environment as well, as the artwork no longer confronts its viewers but takes them within its space of activity. When action rather than representation is its substance, painting no less than sculpture can fill space, and when the viewer is invited to share this presence the primacy of action is complete. Hofmann's model, seen by his students as occupying an all-active space, now shares an environment with the spectator as well: forces within the painting energize the space within which it is seen. Space itself becomes a social concept as revolutionized by Buckminster Fuller, but also by postmodern artists who energize the audience's environment no less than the makers of Fuller's ideal space capsule (*AP*, p. 139). No longer can the public complain that it has been divorced from art, which was the modernist excuse Rosenberg cited in the first edition of *The Tradition of the New*, for now the standard of an artwork's success considers the inclusion of the art public within it. The artist's will acts upon the viewer's imagination, making mind, hand, and canvas one. A correlative of action in the painting is change within the viewer's self, and as such the work proceeds infinitely.

As always, Rosenberg finds a socio-political corollary for what happens in art. Like Roland Barthes, he can trace the initial transformation back to the mid–nineteenth century, even though as a workable aesthetic it has not begun to succeed until postmodern times. The first analogy is to Marx, within whose thought "we have entered a dynamic world dominated no longer by things but by the activities of men." Beyond this one can look back to Hegel, whose concept was "that truth does not reside in essences but is brought into existence by historical events" (AP, p. 220). Rosenberg's *Act and the Actor* collects a career's worth of essays dedicated to finding this principle evident throughout postmodern social and political practice, from Eichmann's performance before the Israeli court to the principles of engagement paramount in current philosophies. The self is formed by acts, and these can claim the force of identity, as in Sartre's and Camus's choices, or of an excuse, as in Eichmann's defense that his actions were part of European history. In Marxism may be found a curious parallel to Eichmann's legal argument, for its philosophy separates principles of activity from individual members, seeing worker and capitalist as mere personifications of behavior and status. The importance of action returns when this philosophy transforms class itself from an economic personification into an historical actor. Philosophy turns into "instigation" as part of the mythical principle "that action can release a foreseen destiny which both dominates existence and precedes thought" (AA, p. 53)—a formulation identical with Rosenberg's explanation of the Action painter at work. Psychoanalytically, this is how Hamlet proceeds, acting "in order to bring about a disclosure, as if he were adding a chemical to a mixture, rather than to achieve a concrete result" (AA, p. 71). The gap between actor and action is, of course, the subject of Shakespeare's play, just as the intransitive nature of the verb *to act* postulates reflexively the character's existence—a reminder of Barthes's belief that for the writer, *to write* is an intransitive verb. The ghost indicates the possibility of a true act, transforming Hamlet's very being on the stage; the character becomes, through action, the author of his self, just as the Action painter exists in the performance of his or her work. "There is no individual until there is an actor," Rosenberg concludes in a formulation applicable to philosophy and to painting, "no concrete existence except in the 'functional relationships.' The play's the thing" (AA, p. 94).

The case is similar in Jean-Paul Sartre's *The Words*, where the writer finds himself on stage and must develop a part for himself in a previously unknown plot. In similar manner André Malraux's career is dedicated to tying himself to a great action of some kind, "united and intoxicated by it" (*AA*, p. 162). In the end, the excuse of an Eichmann becomes the same principle by which his accusers must try him: the fact that Eichmann's speciality, his sole reason for being, removes the crime from the realm of the unspeakable and locates it in history.

An aesthetics of action, of performance, is therefore something quite different from a principle of thought. Against Cubism's ideation of the subject stands Action Painting's work with literal charges of energy, the intellectual explanation and justification for which could follow later. Color action would be more important than color meaning (Hofmann), line would be more interesting than anything it was meant to depict (Pollock), and even the materials of representation themselves would take second place to the artist's action with them, even to the point of Claes Oldenburg's challenge of seeing how far he could extend the estrangement of the familiar without letting it become something different. This way the environment can never become monotonous, thanks to the artist's action within it. Opposed to modernism's exhaustion is the postmodern sense that since life is action and reality is system, there need be no end to creative play.

When action is replaced by activity, Action Painting becomes environmental art, and this increased importance for process makes the canvas surface an even busier area. The artist must now animate that plane of action, making it a dynamic field that responds to succeeding marks placed upon it. The sculptor does the same with space, stressing his or her activity within displaced volume: witness Anthony Caro's elements which "drift out in sideways movements and backward and forward, like an erratic signature" (*ASM*, p. 66). What seems like a display of afterthought is in fact the liveliness of his activity, all the more impressive because of the massively heavy substances within which his seemingly unhampered creation takes place.

This new conception of action as activity, with its broadly environmental implications, reminds Rosenberg that the principle has changed from one of aesthetics to philosophy, a genuine habit of thought:

> In the history of painting styles since the Renaissance, action is a mode of drawing and of handling pigment that tends to alternate with modes of stillness. Van Gogh is active, Seurat still; Mondrian is still, Soutine active. Action in the art of the past fifty years has, however, aims much broader than style; it seeks a recasting of life,

and it extends painting beyond aesthetics into issues of politics, ethics, psychology, and the future of culture. Indeed, action in twentieth-century art implies a repudiation of aesthetics as an objective. With Mondrian, for example, the equilibrium of tensions produced by relations of color, line, and scale is intended to evoke the intellectual state necessary for a new social order. American Action painting at its inception was a method of creation—not a style or a look that pictures strove to achieve. In some instances, it was not even a method so much as an attitude, an outlook. Theoretically, the canvases of Action painters could be entirely different from one another in appearance, and in fact they have been different. Many are totally abstract; others are landscapes and figures, plus figures in landscapes and landscapes that *are* figures. (*AP*, p. 213)

What unites the apparently different works of Pollock, Hofmann, de Kooning, and Newman is the *act:* "No object, but also no idea. The activity of the artist became, in their opinion, primary" (*AP*, p. 213), from Pollock's contact through Hofmann's push and pull to Newman's presence. The principle also obtains in Aaron Siskind's photographs, which "pluck from fences, beaches, rocks, strips of metal, images of possible canvases as if someone had had the ingenuity to paint them." His photographic work contains the intelligence of painting in the action of his selectivity; by definition a direct communications medium, photography in his hands becomes a simplification of means in order to "concentrate on the act of choice" (*CBR*, p. 10). The reality of art, in Rosenberg's view, has become the reality of creating it, and hence Aaron Siskind can join the fold by making a similar choice in his photographer's art.

The result of such activity is *an event*, the result in Barnett Newman's case of a dramatic struggle with format; in his sculpture content draws not upon scale but upon the idea which suggested scale, as expressed through the broken vertical beam—an embodiment which is an event in the play and place of action, not stasis. Like Action Painting, his "Broken Obelisk" is always happening. Describing de Kooning at work, Rosenberg notes how the artist begins with virtually anything—a daub of color, a letter of the alphabet, the sketch of a nude—and then proceeds to live on the canvas, alert to all possibilities of coherence. Proceeding this way, the canvas accumulates event upon event, taking on body "through the stops and starts of the brush" (*WDK*, p. 15). A single painting can thus go on for months, and bear little resemblance to its earlier state. And once accomplished, the Action Painting event remains within its creative frame. As opposed to the automatism of Surrealism which evoked the data of nature and of memory, Action Painting uses a true spontaneity of event in order to project an entirely new world. Yet this new world exists only within its frame, as a de Kooning "Woman" remains a unique happening with no reference to anything occurring off the canvas.

Even a Barnett Newman painting, where so much less activity seems to be taking place, does not mean but rather meets and engages. The paintings are works he has done, not thought of; human activity dominates the idea, and the painting is that activity's evidence. The originality of human action guarantees that it will be form-making, instead of simply imitative, and the persistence of this belief within the postmodern aesthetic is clarified by art movements which succeed Action Painting. Even Pop Art, whose apparent emphasis on image suggests a different standard entirely, turns back to the "lack of respect for forms" (*AP*, p. 223) which characterizes Abstract Expressionism at its best. Action Painting picks and chooses among available techniques, but always transforms them for its own purposes, many of which speak against that particular technique's original purpose (Hofmann's use of color as a surface dynamic, for example); Pop picks up techniques from the street, as it were—from commercial media—and makes them once more conventional for artistic uses. So too for the Happening, which accepts Action Painting's belief that the creative act is more important than the object created. The Happening achieves an almost ideal independence from the objectivity of an artwork by limiting its presence and duration to the event of its creation—when the Happening ends, there is nothing left. From here Rosenberg finds it an easy and logical step to Conceptual Art, for "Art communicated through documents is a development to the extreme of the Action-painting idea that a painting ought to be considered as a record of the artist's creative processes rather than as a physical object. It is the event of the doing, not the thing done, that is the 'work'" (*DDA*, p. 59). That this last sentence can apply to art movements as broadly various as Action Painting, Pop Art, Happenings, and Conceptual Art speaks for the universality of Rosenberg's understanding within the postmodern aesthetic. It applies to virtually every artistic activity within it, and to virtually no activity outside of it.

"The American Action Painters," Rosenberg's seminal essay on the postmodern aesthetic, concludes with an unhappy look at the other arts. He reserves his last sentence for writers: "So far, the silence of American literature on the new painting all but amounts to a scandal" (*TN*, p. 39). In a later essay Rosenberg analyzes the gap between painting and writing, finding that while painters have developed their art free from the smothering restraints of an official tradition, writers have found a more comfortable place within "the *paterfamilias* of the universities, the quarterlies and the editorial offices" (*TN*, p. 257). Mainstream American literature of the 1950s, with its moral tone and dedication to the social milieu, certainly did not share in the creative revolution being launched by the other arts, and an academic environment pledged to the literary standards of an earlier day may well have shared responsibility. But Rosenberg was not about to call for a revolution outside the terms of writing. "The subversion of literary form cannot be accomplished except by literary means," he understands, and therefore asks for *"an effort essentially formal."* Here was the success of Action Painting: " 'formal' art, in undermining accepted form, has been a powerful agent in dissolving also the social stereotypes maintained by them" (*DP*, p. 12). Hence Soviet censors wisely fear a threat to the Party's image of life from vanguard art, and the academic establishment worries for its standards when an anti-academic style takes hold. The environment which produced Pollock and de Kooning also spawned a revolution within music (Monk, Coltrane, and Mingus, all playing in clubs patronized by these painters) but outside of the accepted literary tradition (Kerouac, Ginsberg, Burroughs); only when the latter attacked literature from within could the formal re-invention take place.

"Any genuine attack on society today must occur on the level of abstraction" (*DP*, p. 207)—this sentiment recognizes the impotence of writing oriented simply toward style and theme, from Beat prose and poetry to Black Humor fiction, and anticipates the formal revolution accomplished by writers in the 1960s who directed their efforts toward the underlying aesthetics of literature, just as the Action painters had transformed painting. When painting is pledged to the representation of anything except its own action, there can be no hope for art as art, and the same case prevails for literature. "Social reality gave way to dramatic mimesis because history did not allow human beings to pursue their own ends" (*TN*, p. 154), and when fiction is required to be a secretary to society, no room remains for the essentially fictive act. Ideally, a poem, story, or novel should not indicate any objective representation but must rather point to "the process in which it originated and to the 'new realities' born within it." Its own subject matter takes place in its very act of "manufacture" (*TN*, p. 121), and this sense of doing does not wait for anything, even for inspiration—the writer must simply "set it into motion" (*TN*, p. 109). The roots for this new aesthetic, the same ones to be exploited by the postmodern generation which follows Rosenberg's belief (Ronald Sukenick, Gilbert Sorrentino, Donald Barthelme), can be found in the work of Wallace Stevens, for whom "American poetry became the poet's act of making his existence real to him" (*TN*, p. 91).

Rosenberg's interest in literature reflects his fear that when art and literature are divorced from one another, both suffer a crucial loss of essence. In 1963 he and Thomas B. Hess founded and edited two numbers of a journal, *Location*, devoted to critiquing literature and art in tandem, and in Rosenberg's editorial prefaces may be found an important index to his aesthetics on which he based his magazine:

> The practice of art as a segregated "discipline" brings to the fore its inherent weaknesses. The weakness of painting and sculpture are in their closeness to decoration, that of literature in its ties to reporting. To oversimplify, painting tends toward empty form, literature toward meaningless fact. When they stand eye to eye, each checks the drift in each other: literature demands that painting achieve emotional and intellectual content; painting shows its impatience with the formal laxity of literature. (*Location* 1:4)

By having the two activities monitor each other, Rosenberg finds that literature can boast nothing similar to painting's act of "liberating the creative processes by elevating them above all preconceived aesthetic objectives." Instead, "For twenty years poetry and fiction have had their goals set by a traditionalist imagination in harmony with the formal conservatism of the mass media" resulting in "an incredible naivete in regard to the processes of composition" (1:5). Because of this failure to examine its own practices, literary criticism has rarely risen above discussions of subject matter. In order to move beyond the "single set of formal assumptions [which] now rules the art of writing," Rosenberg suggests that literature join painting in a "continued trying of its medium" (2:9), which is precisely the aesthetic practiced by *Location*'s managing editor, Donald Barthelme.

Bringing Barthelme to New York (from Houston, where he had directed the Contemporary Arts Museum) may well have been a signal event in developing the literature Rosenberg desired, for by the decade's end Barthelme's novel *Snow White* and volumes of stories collected from *The New Yorker* showed that the literary equivalent of Action Painting was not only possible, but could meet with popular success. *Location* provided the forum for Barthelme's literary aesthetic as well, and his "After Joyce" is an important document for laying down the principles by which a generation's innovative fiction could be understood.

Point by point, Barthelme's arguments reflect Rosenberg's postmodern habit of thought. The subject is "the sticky question of what art is 'about' and the mysterious shift that takes place as soon as one says that art is not about something but *is* something" (2:13), a gloss on Rosenberg's dictum of the canvas being not a space in which to reproduce but an arena in which to act. Barthelme asks what is the nature of this new presence added to the world which no longer represents it but is meant to count among it as equal:

> It speaks of a fundamental placement in relation to the work, that of a voyager in the world coming upon a strange object. The reader reconstitutes the work by his active participation, by approaching the object, tapping it, shaking it, holding it to his ear to hear the roaring within. It is characteristic of the object that it does not declare itself all at once, in a rush of pleasant naivete. Joyce enforces the way in which *Finnegans Wake* is to be read. He conceived the reading to be a lifetime project, the book remaining always *there,* like the landscape surrounding the reader's home or the buildings bounding the reader's apartment. The book remains problematic, unexhausted. (2:14)

Barthelme's interpretation recalls Samuel Beckett's postmodernist reading of Joyce, a Joyce whose unfettered writing had left the mythical groundings of modernism behind: his writing is not *about* something, *it is that something itself*. As Barthelme puts it, Joyce might as well be weaving a blanket of what may be found in a hardware store. "The strangeness of his project is an essential part of it, almost its point. The fabric falls apart, certainly, but where it hangs together we are privileged to encounter a world made new" (2:14). Language is followed wherever it leads, just as the Action painter trusts the implications of paint rather than of design. Writing can always be read in such manner, but the postmodern innovation is that now the writer recognizes this fact and makes the most of it.

The first major piece of fiction Rosenberg, Hess, and Barthelme acquired for *Location* was a section of Kenneth Koch's novel *The Red Robins*. Barthelme describes it in terms aesthetically consonant with Action Painting: that Koch's strategy "is to re-enter the history of the novel and fix upon a particular kind of American sub-literature, that of the Rover Boys, Tom Swift . . . and especially a certain kind of light novel popular around the first World War." These techniques are then deliberately misused to the extent that they are reinvented, furnishing a ground against which the writer's technique can react. "He too dispenses with character, action, plot and fact, dispenses with them by permitting them to proliferate all over the landscape and by resolutely short-circuiting the expected order of things." Sentiment provides an occasion to highlight its handling, just as de Kooning handles texture and color. "There is pure linguistic play with abrupt changes of mood and intentionality," much like Pollock's use of line. And in this demonstration of "a consciousness of the work as object, of the medium as message" (2:16), innovative fiction is born, joining Action Painting in an expression of the postmodern way of making art.

Three

Roland Barthes

To Write

It would be interesting to know at what moment the verb to write *began to be used intransitively, the writer no longer being the one who writes* something, *but the one who writes— absolutely: this shift is certainly the sign of an important change in mentality . . . it is paradoxically at the moment when* to write *seems to become intransitive that its object, under the name* book *or* text, *assumes a special importance* (RL, p. 18). From Roland Barthes's hypothesis that *to write* may be an intransitive verb emerges an aesthetic parallel to Harold Rosenberg's transformation of the idea of painting. Rosenberg suggests that the transition to Action Painting occasioned such a profound change in what art is seen to be that he dates it as an epoch—*at a certain moment*—and Barthes shares in this same sense of emergence. "As soon as the writer ceased to be a witness to the universal, to become the incarnation of a tragic awareness (around 1850)," he claims in his first book, *Writing Degree Zero*, "his first gesture was to choose the commitment of his form, either by adopting or rejecting the writing of his past." The results are momentous, and evocative of Rosenberg's new status for the arts: "This was precisely the time when Literature (the word having come into being shortly before) was finally established as an object" (*WDZ*, p. 3).

The type of work produced by Barthes's intransitive writing is virtually identical in its aesthetic to Rosenberg's Action Painting. As a process of "concretization," it establishes "literature as an object" in which "form became the end-product of craftsmanship, like a piece of pottery or a jewel (one must understand that craftsmanship was here made manifest, that is, it was for the first time imposed on the reader as a spectacle)" (*WDZ*, p. 4). And just as Rosenberg's vision reaches from art to society in general, Barthes's project grows from an initial interest in the dynamics of writing to the textual character of existence as a whole. In this latter guise he is known as a semiologist, seeing the human world in its peculiarly written character—*written* when we consider that word in its sense as a grammar of signs.

Arrangements or structures, as in a grammar, are things which are made, and in Barthes's view they have the same objectivity as the written text. The revolutionary nature of this vision is that once made, the structure's only reality is itself: we perceive in terms of difference rather than of identity. Using the familiar linguistic example, the distinction of *cat* is that its initial consonant is *c* instead of *b* or *r*; the word *cat* is not so much a reality as it is the residue of all other letters it is not. Therefore it is the system and not the thing in itself that constitutes our knowledge of reality. "Of course, structuralism, in one sense, is very old," Barthes admits; "the world is a structure, objects and civilizations are structures, we've known that for a long time. Still, what is entirely new is the perception of this decentration" (*GV*, p. 102), which puts a new emphasis on the arbitrary nature of such ordering.

This structural vision in turn enriches Barthes's perception of literature. Anticipating Ihab Hassan's principal metaphor, he describes its elusive substance: "One could say that literature is Orpheus returning from the underworld; as long as literature walks ahead, aware that it is leading someone, the reality behind it which it is gradually leading out of the unnamed—that reality breathes, walks, lives, heads toward the light of a meaning; but once literature turns around to look at what it loves, all that is left is a named meaning, which is a dead meaning" (*CE*, p. 268). Literature may use the same processes of signification as does routine language, but when viewed structurally this writing assumes a double sense of artifice. It is not the things but the place of things that matters, Barthes insists, and his distinction gives prominence to the inventive qualities of both literature and the language in which it happens. Like Abstract Expressionist painting, structure contains activity. Its goal is "to reconstruct an 'object' in such a way as to manifest thereby the rules of functioning (the 'functions') of this object" (*CE*, p. 214). Truth is no longer to be sought in depth, but in extent; it is not a kernel at the center of a work, but the very texture and tissue out of which it is made—not a nut to crack, but an onion to peel.

Literature presents a distinct challenge, however, since its materials signify in their normal course of being. Painting can be made realistic through credible depiction, but the daubs of paint do not have to mean anything beyond themselves and the painter's action with them—this was the formal triumph of Action Painting. But no matter how they are used, once on the page words refer to their signified object, quite apart from the writer's intention: "forever doomed to signify itself just when it wants to signify the world, literature is a motionless object, separated by a world in the making" (*CE*, p. 267). Certain literary forms have a successful tradition of escaping this necessary signification, such as the haiku, whose "task is to achieve exemption from meaning within a perfectly readerly discourse (a contradiction denied to Western art, which can contest meaning only by rendering its discourse incomprehensible)" (*EmS*, p. 81). Western literature takes an opposite direction, toward what Barthes calls a bourgeois economy of value which centralizes meaning as a commodity of exchange. When literature is not distinguished from customarily signifying language (in which meaning is perforce a matter of bonded identification between word and represented object), the reader's instinctive enjoyment is held in bondage by an acculturated, determined practice. As Richard Howard says in his translator's headnote, "Only when we know—and it is a knowledge gained by taking pains, by renouncing what Freud calls instinctual gratification—what we are doing when we read, are we free to enjoy what we read. As long as our enjoyment is—or is said to be—instinctive it is not enjoyment, it is terrorism" (*SZ*, p. ix).

The Japanese haiku offers a different strategy, and Barthes recalls that it is in his study of Japanese culture, *Empire of Signs,* that he begins considering the pleasure of the text. Signs can be the joy of literature, but they can also be its oppressors, and in such works as the haiku writers and readers find the proper balance between signification and structure: "I cannot tolerate languages or societies that neutralize signs: they 'live' the signs but refuse to proclaim them as such. In other words, they do not experience the signs for what they are: products of history, ideological elaborations of meaning. This intolerance was the spark for my *Mythologies,* for example" (*GV*, p. 158). Japan offers strong codes which resist the naturalization so prevalent in a bourgeois culture, the culture of mass media and statist propaganda which produces the world Barthes so deftly deconstructs in *Mythologies* and *The Eiffel Tower*. When signifieds are ultimately stable and closed, the sign-making relationship ossifies and the sign can never show itself off as sign. But what has interested Barthes is the way people make the world intelligible to themselves, and such knowledge involves a defabrication of the sign system to show how signs function in creating a useable reality. People give meanings, not words, and once so endowed, writing creates a meaning not present in those words before. Literature which casts doubt on the meaning of things—be it the Japanese haiku or the French nouveau roman—is Barthes's favorite. In such work "The object appears without the halo of meanings, and that is what gives birth to anxiety, which is a profound, and metaphysical, feeling" (*GV*, p. 10). A writer such as Alain Robbe-Grillet and the critic Roland Barthes strip objects of their usual significance, inaugurating a new way of looking at the object, and in this project is found a postmodern habit of thought.

Barthes's greatest nemesis is the "naturalization of the cultural," a process which results when "the text loads the image, burdening it with a culture, a moral, an imagination" (*IMT,* p. 26; *RF*, pp. 14–15). He takes great exception to the practice of hiding a constructed meaning under the appearance of a given meaning, because such denotation naturalizes the message, making it innocent of the complex artifice of connotation and creating a pseudo-truth with the status of a natural object. When the code by which a construction has been produced is disguised, the message is disintellectualized because it establishes in nature the arbitrary constraints of a culture. It is interesting to note that Barthes sees true meaning being lost when the codes are lost; what those codes imply is beside the point, except as a deception which his deconstructive act unmasks. As with Action Painting, the point and truth are in the doing, and if that doing is effaced, all is lost.

Hence the crisis of a postmodern society unwilling to live by its vitalizing aesthetic. An at least implicit recognition of codes is needed for this society to operate; virtually everything is determined by "a corpus of rules that are so worn we take them to be marks of nature; but if the narrative departed from them, it would very rapidly become unreadable" (*UT*, p. 156). Yet at the same time a reluctance to declare such codes characterizes bourgeois society and the mass culture it produces, a culture which employs signs which do not look like signs but rather as natural facts. Hence the crisis in authenticity Rosenberg and others found in the modernist view. To pretend that a cultural order is natural and reasonable creates a passion for meaning that feeds itself on objects which in fact mean nothing, such as fashion and sports; in this same manner true signs become invisible simply by the fact of their pervasive presence. The understanding of art suffers when such mythologies are used as alibis for reality, and so both as a literary and social critic Barthes dedicates himself to "discomfit what is supposedly natural" (*GV*, p. 318).

In his autobiography Barthes explains the "ethnological temptation" which in its range characterizes his life's work:

> What pleased him in Michelet is the foundation of an ethnology of France, the desire and the skill of questioning historically—i.e., *relatively*—those objects supposedly the most natural: face, clothes, complexion. Elsewhere the population of Racine's tragedies, and that of Sade's novels, have been described as tribed, as closed ethnic groups whose structure must be studied. In his *Mythologies,* it is France itself which is ethnographed. Further, he has always loved the great novelistic cosmogonies (Balzac, Zola, Proust), so close to little societies. This is because the ethnological book has all the powers of the beloved book: it is an encyclopedia, noting and classifying all of reality, even the most trivial, the most

sensual aspects; this encyclopedia does not adulterize the Other by reducing it to the Same; appropriation diminishes, the Self's certitude grows lighter. Finally, of all learned discourse, the ethnological seems to come closest to a Fiction. (*RB*, pp. 84–85)

Barthes's joy in exposing the natural not as an attribute of Physical Nature but as the alibi of a social majority, "a legality" (*RB*, p. 130), does reveal a fictionalizing to the extent that he uncovers *"Language worked on by power,"* a system in which stereotypes are produced as fictive artifices but are then "consumed as innate meanings" (*BR*, p. 471). The critic's semiology uncovers this fictive impulse and restores it as a matter for appreciation, at the same time protecting society from the delusion which would be worked upon it. "Culture, in all its aspects, is a language," Barthes finds, and his task is to learn its system of grammar. "Discourse is not only a sum of sentences," he emphasizes; "it is, itself, one great sentence" (*RL*, p. 13), and learning how to read is his task.

Dismantling this language is Barthes's pleasant task. It is an acknowledgment of the pleasure of the text (which depends upon a revelation of its working), and a recognition that "Any considerable rupture of the everyday introduces Festivity" (*ET*, p. 31). The opposite of Festivity or Carnival is, as Julia Kristeva shows, Monology, a system of imposed, monolithic authority, and it fits right in with Barthes's manner of study that Japan, his empire of signs, does not partake in the monological discourse so common to the Western world. In the West we have what Barthes calls "the Don Juanism of the text" (*GV*, p. 159), and unraveling its seductive practice is a key to its fictive nature. Once Barthes can find its systematics, which is the play of the system behind it, he can recover the dialogical principle which naturalization has transformed into a monology of order.

The great advantage of Barthes's method, and an indication that it touches a central principle of postmodern thought, is that it works equally well for specific literary questions (where the results are more easily certifiable) as it does for social practice at large. For each, Barthes's first task is to locate "the very materiality of the signifier" (*UT*, p. 33) which in literature is the text and in society is the code by which things function. This materiality is a realm of interaction—not the subject, nor the language which expresses it, but rather the signifying practice where the two meet. Signification is not produced at the level of abstraction but through the very operation of its practice. This notion of signifying practice restores active energy to language and makes any linguistic or social action as interesting as fiction. The text is a tissue, something woven—one thinks of Donald Barthelme's characterization of Joyce's late, postmodernist work as a weaving which deliberately unravels in its reading—and the fabric of this texture comes from the interlacing of codes which the semiologist separates into its component parts. Barthes's textual analysis does not simply note a structure, but produces a mobile structuration of the text which locates its avenues of meaning. "What founds the text is not an internal, closed accountable structure," which would as such be a kernel of meaning extractable by the critic—the very act of naming which kills Orpheus's beloved object—but rather the study of "the outlet of the text on to other texts, other codes, other signs; what makes the text is the intertextual" (*UT,* p. 137), the interwoven strands of which the critic must sort out. It is in the interest of each narrative to delay this unweaving, to prolong its existence in suspense which exists not as a flat, tabular space but as "a volume, a stereophony" (*UT,* p. 157) which its temporary irresolution fills.

When Barthes advocates a literature, it is one which makes his same arguments. Among his earliest essays are polemical pieces in favor of the nouveau roman as written by Robbe-Grillet, specifically because his writing "has no alibi, no density and no depth; it remains on the surface of the object and inspects it impartially, without favoring any particular quality" (*CE,* p. 14). While traditionally realistic literature practices the bourgeois economy of cloaking itself in implied judgments, Robbe-Grillet's work sets up an optical resistance which destroys the adjective—qualifications are spatial and never analogical, for in the structuralization of analogies lies the great subterfuge the critic must unmask. Proceeding from the innovations of Robbe-Grillet, Barthes finds in Michel Butor's *Mobile* an even more encompassing technique, that of making the general schema of his work count for nothing at all, while raising detail to the rank of structure, distributing ideas rather than developing them so that they might exist without characterization. Butor structures his book according to the alphabet, a degree zero of classification which voids any a priori sense of value. Among the newest writers, Barthes advocates the work of Philippe Sollers, finding in a novel such as *H* a tactic much like Action Painting which effectively keeps the seductions of language in control:

> *H* constitue donc un certain procès de la Phrase. Et cependant, ce qui est substitué à la Phrase, ce n'est pas son contraire mécanique, le babil, la bouillie. Une troisième forme apparaît, qui garde de la phrase sa séduction langagière, mais évite sa découpe, sa clôture, c'est-à-dire, en définitive, son *pouvoir de représentation*. *H* tisse, non des phrases, mais des mouvements syntaxiques, des bribes d'intelligibilité, des taches de langage (au sens que ce mot pourrait avoir dans la calligraphie d'un Pollock). (*SE*, pp. 62–63)

> *H* then constitutes a certain trying of the sentence. However, that which is substituted in the sentence isn't its opposite device, prattle, pulp. A third form appears, which retains the linguistic seduction of the sentence but avoids its indentation, its closure, in other words, definitely, its power of representation. *H* weaves not sentences but syntactical movements, scraps of intelligibility, drips of language (in the sense that this word can have in the calligraphy of a Pollock).

Sollers therefore directs attention back to language itself, instead of letting the usual systems of mediation—money, phallus, concept—work their determinations on our history.

Barthes's own work as a critic follows Robbe-Grillet's and others as writers: a practice of his talents upon the surface of language, ever mindful of the abyss of naturalized meaning into which the inattentive reader can fall. Thinking back to the first writer he studied, Barthes remarks of himself that "he does with Michelet what he claims Michelet has done with historical substance: he functions by sliding over the entire surface, he caresses" (*RB*, p. 58). The method is perfectly self-reflexive, as the identical form of Seuil's "Ecrivains de Toujours" series can be used for Barthes's *Michelet par lui-même* (1954) and for his own *Roland Barthes par Roland Barthes* (1975). In each, the author follows a brief bibliographically oriented survey of his subject with a collection of glosses on key words. For Michelet, these begin with "Migraines," "Travail" [Work], "Michelet malade d'Histoire" [a person sick from history], "J'ai hâte" [I'm in a hurry], "Michelet marcheur" [the walker], "Michelet nageur" [the swimmer], "Le Survol" [the skimmer]; for Barthes, the key terms begin with "Active/ reactive," "The adjective," "Ease," "The demon of analogy," "On the blackboard," "Money," and "The ship *Argo*." This organizational plan separates these terms from the ongoing discourse of the writer's life, where various mediating devices might direct them toward systematic meanings, and holds them separate as objects. To enhance this sense of individuality, Barthes organizes his own book (in the original French) by a structure so self-consciously obvious that it means everything and therefore nothing—the alphabet—and which can accomplish no mediation of meaning. Whether alphabetical or topical, the structure of singling out these words opens the door for the author himself to speak; framed by Barthes's categories and introductory comments, quotes from Michelet are allowed to speak for themselves—hence the book's title, *Michelet par lui-même* [Michelet by himself]. In *Roland Barthes par Roland Barthes* there is no need for the author to cite himself, for the technique has allowed the same opportunity: by taking key words out of the context which would otherwise smooth them over in a rush toward meaning, the author is allowed to speak them with a savor of themselves. So spoken, their weight within his own writing is preserved, instead of being surrendered to the system of meaning constructed by others around him.

Such disassembly, even of the most mechanical sort, is necessary to escape the determinations of language. "In fact, today, there is no language site outside bourgeois ideology: our language comes from it, returns to it, remains closed up in it," Barthes warns, and reveals that therefore "I listen to the message's transport, not the message" (*SFL*, p. 10). Hence his interest in another early subject, *The Fashion System*, because, unlike language practiced by society, fashion's "*only goal is to disappoint the meaning it luxuriously elaborates:* the system then abandons the meaning yet does so without giving up any of the spectacle of signification," which Barthes at once identifies as "a process (as opposed to *meaning*)." Fashion is "an exemplary form of the general act of signification, thus rejoining the very being of literature" (*FS*, pp. 288–89)—an especially valuable model when one considers how society's naturalization of codes imposes itself on the products of fiction, poetry, and drama.

Seeing how the fashion system works is a reminder of how creatively the system of literary signification should be allowed to function.

Cy Twombly, "Synopsis of a Battle," 1968. Collection of the Virginia Museum of Fine Arts. Gift of Sydney and Frances Lewis.

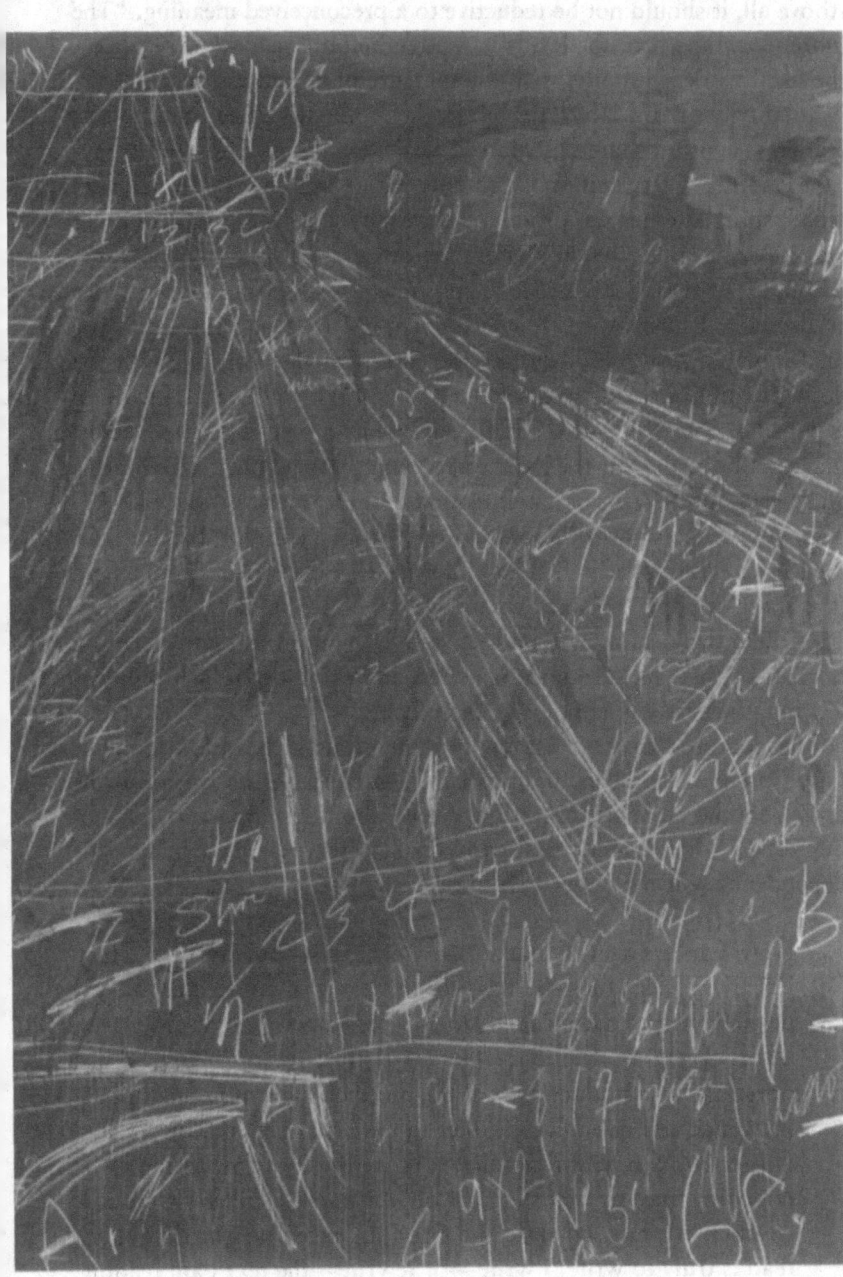

53
Roland
Barthes:
To Write

Above all, it should not be reductive to a preconceived meaning. "The more plural the text, the less it is written before I read it" (*SZ*, p. 10); the ideal work is infinite, with the measure of its success no longer in its finality but in the labor it exhibits, the production it engenders in its readers—a vision shared by Harold Rosenberg in his definition of Action Painting. Composition is "to offer for *doing*" (*RF*, p. 265), an act which shifts attention to production; reviewing painter Cy Twombly's work, Barthes finds that he "summons, attracts the spectator: he wants to join the canvas, not in order to consume it aesthetically, but in order to produce it in his turn (to 'reproduce' it)" (*RF*, p. 191), exploring one's comparative impotence in contrast with the artist's power—a desire, in other words, "to do *the same thing*" (*RF*, p. 192). If anything is consumed, it is the artist's body, and what is seen is a retrospective movement, "what was the hand's *becoming*." As for the reality of this affair, it is "the *process* of manipulation, not the object produced" (*RF*, p. 172); Twombly's work does not derive from a concept, the mark on the canvas, "but from an activity (*marking*); or better still: from a field (the sheet of paper), insofar as an activity is deployed there" (*RF*, p. 173). Like the fashion system, this style of painting is appreciated by Barthes because its substance is action, a writing "of which only the leaning, the cursivity remains" (*RF*, p. 164).

The notion of process has many dimensions in Barthes's thought. Like Rosenberg's understanding of the same term, it derives from the critic's special emphasis on action. Asked about his apparently greater interest in what readers (as opposed to writers) do, he explains the dependency which a concern with process fosters:

> Now, I am convinced that a theory of reading (that reading which has always been the poor relation of literary creation) is absolutely dependent on a theory of writing: to read a text is to discover—on a corporeal, not a conscious level—*how it was written,* to invest oneself in the production, not the product. This movement of coincidence can be initiated either in the usual fashion, by pleasurably reliving the poetics of the work, or in a more modern way, by removing from oneself all forms of censorship to allow the text the freedom of all its semantic and symbolic excesses; at this point, to read is truly to write: I write—or rewrite—the text I am reading, even better and more searchingly than its author did. (*GV*, p. 189)

Such an activist mode of reading alerts us to the signifying practice at hand, and this practice restores energy to language. By remembering that the text is a productivity, the reader can meet it in the very theatre of production; the fact that this text is written on the page does not mean that it stops working, any more than an action painting becomes a static work once completed. Desire is here the key activating element, for in full reading the reader becomes one who desires to write and who surrenders to "an erotic practice of language" in sympathy with what is happening in the text itself: those "perpetual productions, enunciations, through which the subject continues to struggle" (*UT*, p. 42). Being read, the text never stops, and certainly cannot close. There is no final signified.

This is why Barthes credits theatre as the crossroads of his oeuvre, since spectacle is the universal category in which the world is seen, specifically the act of signaling that places signs in motion. The text can be experienced only in an activity of production, which is its practice of an infinite deferment of the signified within the field of the signifier, the infinity of which makes it the ideal plaything. Hence Barthes's appreciation, in his first published essay, of Gide, who "puts everything in the *movement* of his thought and not in its brutal profession" (*BR*, p. 8), and his lifelong enjoyment in narrative of "not directly its content, or even its structure, but rather the abrasions I impose upon the fine surface: I read on, I skip, I look up, I drop in again" (*PT*, pp. 11–12), all in an activist mode. Eventually this measure of action leads to two styles of reading:

> Text of pleasure: the text that contents, fills, grants euphoria; the text that comes from culture and does not break with it, is linked to a *comfortable* practice of reading. Text of bliss [*jouissance*]: the text that imposes a state of loss, the text that discomforts (perhaps to the point of a certain boredom), unsettles the reader's historical, cultural, psychological assumptions, the consistency of his tastes, values, memories, brings to a crisis his relation with language. (*PT*, p. 14)

Because of its working power, this latter text actively desires the reader, paralleling the reader's desire of the text; the product of all this activity is *signifiance*, which is meaning only insofar as it is sensually produced.

Cy Twombly, "Untitled," 1969. Collection of the Whitney Museum of American Art. Gift of Mr. and Mrs. Rudolph B. Schulhof.

57
Roland
Barthes:
To Write

Barthes's emphasis on production, like Rosenberg's, follows the same course of interest through surface, plastic activity, and material. He studies Cy Twombly's work to find out that what seems to be writing is actually an activity "born from the surface itself" (*RF*, p. 162), thanks to the artist's interest in activity rather than in expressing a concept. The graphic event is, after all, what allows the paper's surface to exist and to signify, and such pleasurable practice is the same motive Rosenberg found in Action Painting. The plasticity of this act upon the surface is a matter of both time and space, the painter's brush or the writer's pen implying both a past and a future within the presence of its touch; both memory and anticipation figure in its action. By this line of activity creation displaces itself, making the object of desire (the page or canvas) its subject: "it is an *energon*, a labor which reveals—which makes legible—the trace of its pulsion and its expenditure. The line is visible action" (*RF*, p. 170). Again, the evidence is not of a product but of process, of the hand's becoming, and the effect of that becoming is measured not in the finality of the text or canvas "but in the labor it exhibits (the production of which it seeks to bear in its 'reader')" (*RF*, p. 227). As a result, the artist's and the writer's materials exist not as something to service a purpose "but as an absolute substance, manifested in its glory." The materials prevail as substance, seen as themselves rather than as windows through which something else may be viewed; the artist does not flaunt substance, but will "permit it to linger" (*RF*, p. 178) in a way which reveals its essence.

What Rosenberg has done for paint in the postmodern idiom, Barthes has done for language. Whereas other aesthetics might let the two become invisible or at least transparent, Barthes shows that "language never ceases to accompany discourse, holding up to it the mirror of its own structure" (*IMT*, p. 85), just as for Rosenberg every work of Action Painting was a trace of the artist's activity with paint. In writing, certain forms highlight this process: the haiku, as we have seen, and the lover's discourse, which exists as "a solitude of system": "I am alone in making a system out of it (perhaps because I am ceaselessly flung back on the solipsism of my discourse). A difficult paradox: I can be understood by everyone (love comes from books, its dialect is a common one), but I can be heard (received 'prophetically') only by subjects who have *exactly* and *right now* the same language I have" (*LD*, p. 212). The lovers' dialogue is self-consciously structural, each argument exchanged with a sense of symmetry yet in a way which raises the bid; just like the sentence, its structure invites modification and development, each to infinite degrees. Language, like mankind, expands forever, and one becomes a hero simply by having the last word. "I love you" is a statement effected by the need to receive the formulaic response "I love you, too." What the lover wants is language itself, "to *obtain the word*" (LD, p. 153). Hence the phrase is not a sign but a play against sign which evokes a recognition of the language system, just the self-apparency Barthes demands for an understanding of discourse and Rosenberg expects in an appreciation of painting. It is structure which constitutes identity, and Barthes is drawn to metaphors which show this: the haiku, the lover's discourse, the fashion system, and any other number of systems which remind him of the ship *Argo*:

> each piece of which the Argonauts gradually replaced, so that they ended with an entirely new ship, without having to alter either its name or its form. This ship Argo is highly useful: it affords the allegory of an eminently structural object, created not by genius, inspiration, determination, evolution, but by two modest actions (which cannot be caught up in any mystique of creation): *substitution* (one part replaces another, as in a paradigm) and *nomination* (the name is in no way linked to the stability of the parts): by dint of combinations made within one and the same name, nothing is left of the *origin: Argo* is an object with no other cause than its name, with no other identity than its form. (RB, p. 46)

Barthes's formulation is linguistic, recalling Saussure's understanding of language as system, not identity: the 8:25 p.m. Geneva-Paris express is considered the same train every day, even though the chances of it consisting of the same cars and locomotive are minimal. For these same reasons Barthes appreciates music, which like signifying derives not from a metalanguage but from a discourse of parts, just like a lover's discourse in which relationships are conveyed without articulating any other meaning, a virtual syntax without semiotics in which the order of units, rather than any single unit, signifies.

"A language is therefore a horizon," Barthes states at the beginning of his first book, "and style a vertical dimension, which together map out for the writer a Nature, since he does not choose either" (WDZ, p.

Cy Twombly, "The Italians," 1961. Collection of the Museum of Modern Art, New York. Blanchette Rockefeller Fund.

61
Roland
Barthes:
To Write

13). A vocabulary becomes poetic thanks to usage, not invention, and by selecting structures which remind us of this choice—such as alphabetical ordering—Barthes establishes the notion of a *degree zero* of writing. This status "refers to the utopia of a lifting of signs, an exemption from meaning, an indivision of language, a transparency of social relations" (*GV*, p. 195). Such writing, while pregnant with future meaning, is an indicative mood not overlaid by commitments to form and to history. Barthes finds functioning examples of this degree zero everywhere, most notably in the Eiffel Tower: "It participates in no rite, in no cult, not even in Art; you cannot visit the Tower as a museum: there is nothing to see *inside* the Tower" (*ET*, p. 7), yet it is the ideal place from which *to* see. He finds it also in the language of Saint Ignatius Loyola, whose *Journal* strives for a Divine dialogue in which God speaks but does not mark, making "the withholding of the mark itself into an ultimate sign," a sign absorbed in its hearing—an "empty and yet significant place called the degree zero of the sign" (*SFL*, p. 75). Even Racine provides, through his very transparency, a "critical object at zero degree, a site empty but eternally open to signification" (*OR*, pp. viii–ix). His practice evokes Barthes's sense of the photograph, which reproduces infinitely something which has happened only once, yet in which "the event is never transcended for the sake of something else" (*CL*, p. 4). The photo is equally resistant to any reductive system, and cannot be transformed because "it is wholly ballasted by the contingency of which it is the weightless, transparent envelope" (*CL*, p. 5). It is simply an indication to look, to see, a materialization of the phrase *Voila!* Whatever expansion there is must happen by metonymy, not metaphor; like the image of the self which can be found only in one's mother, the degree zero Barthes idealizes is an acknowledgment that something has been present and yet immediately separated, a quality which we will see him eventually describing as novelistic.

Writing degree zero may be an ideal, but it is a necessary one. If everything is allowed to signify, the writer is entrapped, bound in calculations that are not his or her own; the writer is kept from enjoyment. Pleasure, on the other hand, suspends the signified value in writing, shifting value to the signifier. Robbe-Grillet's nouveau roman seeks this pleasure in purifying narrative objects as a zero-theme of plot—*making* the crime in his suspense story, not betraying it, and thus remaining literal. By having his novelistic universe cohere by means of objects alone, Robbe-Grillet avoids the metalanguages of imposed meaning which would lift his narrative's action out of the text and place it in the rarified realm of subjective projections. Rejecting story, anecdote, and the psychology of motivation is a matter of disallowing the signification of objects. That signification, we shall see, is a language unto itself, for which a semiotics of culture is demanded for an adequate translation and comprehension.

Once Barthes has established the zero degree of writing, he can show how other languages are built upon its structure, each with its own layering of meaning. The advantage is that now meaning can be exposed for the artifice it is; rather than a fully natural phenomenon, these systems can be seen with their human impositions and cultural restraints in action. *Mythologies* and *The Eiffel Tower and Other Mythologies* (originally one book in France) are the repositories for these studies of *metalanguage,* a term Barthes uses because it lets him speak about the base language *as language* without the distraction of considering its content. Seeing myth as metalanguage reveals that it is "speech *stolen and restored,*" with Barthes's investigations showing how this restored speech "is no longer quite that which was stolen: when it was brought back, it was not put exactly in its place. It is this brief act of larceny, this moment taken for a surreptitious faking, which gives mythical speech its benumbed look" (M, p. 125). In this process of taking and returning, a second level of language is introduced, the transformation of history into nature and of meaning into form. Myth is always language robbery, Barthes attests, and warns that nothing is safe from it. It masks what is essentially a semiological system as an inductive end, and makes equivalence imply a causal structure, naturalizing the relationship between signifier and signified into a system of authority. What is in fact a set of values is accepted as a system of facts, making what is really a metalanguage prevail as language itself.

Ultimately the controller of language controls the world, and the operations Barthes describes are matters of power: "The oppressed *makes* the world, he has only an active, transitive (political) language; the oppressor conserves it, his language is plenary, intransitive, gestural, theatrical: it is Myth. The language of the former aims at transforming, of the latter at eternalizing" (M, p. 149). This eternalization is how bourgeois ideology turns the products of history into essential types; its favorite forms are the proverb and the maxim, tautological statements which have no demonstrative value but which nevertheless exercise "a certain tyranny of *likelihood*" (*ET*, p. 111). The critic's role is to discover the "friction" (*CE*, p. 258) between the two languages operating in all such statements. Barthes makes the distinction by looking back to the photograph: at degree zero it can be read as a pure sign whose perfect legibility of form does not disorganize us in its reading, but when dressed up with posed attitudes adds a note of challenge—and here is where the metalanguage takes over. It is such language which gives the depicted event "the epic promotion which allows it to be solidified" (*ET*, p. 84), but which in fact postulates a reality all its own. Such are Barthes's favorite examples among his mythologies as an ethnography of modern-day France, from the bourgeois ideal of sentimental poetry to the women's advice columns which postulate only a parasitical condition (marriage), giving her no real access to the world. Metalanguages being mistaken for base language itself is another example of cultural naturalization, and one more level of estrangement of life from reality.

There is only one pure language, and that is of the alphabet: "language before discourse, language before the syntagm, and yet, already, by the letter's substitutive richness, entirely open to the treasures of the symbol" (*RF*, p. 120). Such pure intelligibility, however, can be sterile, as in the alphabet used only for ordering or, as Barthes notes astutely from social practice, from the signal nature of the cover girl in fashion, who is "too busy constituting herself as a sign" (*RF*, p. 114) to be much good as an object for fantasy. It is what is done with signification that becomes interesting, even if it makes us liable to entrapment. This is what makes fashion more complex than the highway code: its exercise in discourse. The key is to isolate metalanguage from the language beneath it, so that the operations of meaning can be seen as just that—as operations, artifices which have no natural claim to being. It is in this manner that Barthes finds the sentence to be an object unto itself: it is an identifiable object thanks not to its meaning (which is variable) but to its structure, and since there are good and bad structures the sentence does have an attribute by which it can be characterized. This is why Barthes "idolizes" the sentence, for within it he can exercise "the individuation, the scent, the seduction, the fetishism of language"

(*BR*, p. 482), all of which are highlighted by the sentence's transparency of structure.

Isolating the forms and functions of the collective imagination rather than its themes has long been Barthes's goal, the project for which involves a description of language characterized by its signifiers rather than by its signifieds. This activity forms his ethic of sign and meaning, an attempt to isolate the empty sign which by "extraordinary finesse . . . doesn't refer to anything" (*GV*, p. 83), an operation leaving nothing to the nonsign. Barthes finds such a practice in Japan, where "a system that is almost entirely immersed in the signifier thrives on the perpetual retreat of the signified" (*GV*, p. 84), and which thus presents no problems of a metalanguage naturalizing itself as meaning. With no system of monotheism, Japan has no supreme signified to anchor the chain of signs, and without such an anchor the signs are allowed to flaunt themselves freely and be savored for their own delight. Monotheism, on the other hand, is the prime example of a constraint which halts the play of signs and directs a meaning. Signs are thus neutralized, but never in an acknowledged fashion that attests to the monology at hand; discourse is directed covertly.

True writing begins with the signifier, and in order to be serious about investigating discourse, that is where the critic must begin, using style as an indication. One can remain here forever, and indeed that is what writing intends, as the text is able to send the reader from one signifier to another without ever closing itself off. It is not a question of creating signs (the business of meaning), but of combining them— hence Barthes's appreciation of Arcimboldo's paintings, the signifying materials of which remain, by design, themselves (such as a face composed of fruits and vegetables), and therefore constitute painting as "a veritable language" (*RF*, p. 134):

> Thus, Arcimboldo imposes a system of substitution (an apple comes to stand for a cheek, as in a coded message; a letter or a syllable comes to mask another letter or another syllable), and, in the same way, a system of transposition (the whole figure is somehow drawn back toward the detail). However, and this is Arcimboldo's peculiarity, what is remarkable about the composite heads is that the picture *hesitates* between coding and decoding: even

> when we have displaced the screen of substitution and of transposition in order to perceive the head composed as an *effect*, our eyes retain the tracery of the first meanings which have served to produce this effect. (*RF*, p. 137)

By speaking this double language, Arcimboldo makes the critic's job easier; the process he dramatizes in his paintings is just what Barthes strives to uncover in all the operations of metalanguage.

As in Harold Rosenberg's appreciation of painting, Barthes finds that these operations are seen best when isolated as actions. Highlighting such activity in turn establishes not just a new perspective, but lays the grounds for an entirely new conception of the thing in question. Just as Rosenberg sees the artwork less as a product and more as a process in action, Barthes views matters such as literature and the fashion system as occasions of activity. Fashion exists only as discourse, he insists, and even in the most precise applications of its activity he sees that it is the name and not the object that creates desire as the system's motivator. In a similar way, literature "*stages* language instead of simply using it" (*BR*, p. 463), taking knowledge not just for its own transparent function but as an integer to be fed into a machine of infinite reflexivity, the purpose of which is to make knowledge "festive" (*BR*, p. 464).

Literature enacts signs, rather than just consuming (and hence destroying) them as knowledge. By this same principle the piece of clothing is by the fashion system transformed into a "written garment" (*FS*, p. 3), the being of which resides fully in its linguistic, systematic meaning. The sociology of fashion may well be directed toward real clothing to be sold and worn, but what Barthes distinguishes as its semiology is directed solely to a system of collective representations:

> it is not the cape which signifies, it is its assertion: meaning denies substance all intrinsic value. This denial is perhaps the most profound function of the Fashion system; contrary to language, this system on the one hand must deal with substance (clothing) encumbered by extra-semantic uses, and on the other hand it has absolutely no need to make use of a combinative relay, like that of the double articulation, since its signifieds are in fact very few in number. . . . Fashion thus appears essentially—and this is the final definition of its economy—as a system of signifiers, a classi-

ficatory activity, much more a semiological than a semantic order. (*FS*, pp. 279–80)

The semiological reality of fashion approaches that of literature, as the simple references to "*spring, weekend, cocktails* become divinities which seem to produce the garment naturally, instead of remaining with it in an arbitrary relation of signification" (*FS*, p. 282). Mobile signification yields to an immediate sacralization of the sign, as signified and signifier are separated but yet stick together as if by natural law. It is here that fashion joins literature as an activity which reads not the meaning of things but their relative positions in a system of signals, which Barthes sees as the most characteristically human activity: mankind as the sign-making animal. It is therefore appropriate that this activity have its full set of analytical classifications—*clothing*'s structural form as a language, with the particulars of *dress* as speech—which can produce a sign (Barthes's example is the sign *Prints win at the races,* in which the vestimentary signifier *prints* combines with the worldly signified *the races*).

It is of the greatest importance that signs be available for this discourse. Without them, communication is weighted down by the ponderous exchange of things themselves, as in the comic spectacle of cavemen talking by picking up and moving items themselves instead of signaling them by name. The signal nature of the fashion system is that it makes discourse about styles of dress practical for a woman, who can multiply her person without any loss of self. Fashion is not play itself, but the sign of play; not a game of being, but "simply a keyboard of signs from among which an external person chooses one day's amusement; it is the final luxury of a personality rich enough to be multiplied, stable enough never to be lost" (*FS*, p. 257).

The elemental principle that the sign is not the thing itself has profound implications for Barthes's contribution to the postmodern habit of thought. Like Rosenberg's distinction that it is not the painting but the painter's action which constitutes the work of art, Barthes's emphasis on the sign's workings relocates human activity, giving systematics a new privilege. It is not revolutionary for Barthes to view literature or fashion as systems, but when he approaches an entire civilization this way, as he does in *Empire of Signs,* it is. His strategy is to choose a culture unlike his own, especially far away, as a way of isolating "a certain number of features (a term employed in linguistics), and out of these features deliberately form a system. It is this system which I shall call: Japan" (*EmS*, p. 3). By doing so Barthes finds that food, for example, need no longer be handled simply as food, but as something established "within a reduced system of substance . . . in a shimmer of the signifier," all of which contributes to "a profound space which hierarchizes man, table, and universe" (*EmS*, p. 14). If a sign is an envelope for meaning, Barthes's system shows how "from envelope to envelope, the signified flees"; a compensatory emphasis on packaging (as opposed to content) means that "the pleasure, the field of the signifier, has been taken: the package is not empty, but emptied" (*EmS*, p. 46). To search for the object which is packaged would be to discard the sign, which in this system is the actual locus of value (as it is in the fashion system and in literature, each of which Barthes has established as a privileged area of human activity). In similar terms the mechanics of Japanese drama highlight its theatricality (the drama's reason for being), by which "the signifier does nothing but turn itself inside out, like a glove" (*EmS*, p. 49). The work of dramatics is thereby substituted for any inwardness of meaning.

Barthes admires Japanese culture in particular, and self-apparent sign systems in general, because of their textural nature—"the *inside* no longer commands the *outside*" (*EmS*, p. 62). This is the same principle Rosenberg uses to establish the aesthetic of Action Painting, and Barthes joins him in an appreciation of the surface as a locus of human activity. Both regret the deciphering which must take place in Western culture to reach this plane. In French the common term is *déchiffrement*, "decoding," an honorable enough profession and certainly a necessary one in its English usage, but which in Barthes's native language recalls the term *chiffonnier*, which means "rag-picker." A negative connotation Barthes himself explores is that of *piercing* meaning— "to get into it by breaking and entering" (*EmS*, p. 72), as opposed to the Japanese reader's ability to let language reveal its essence in its handling. And this handling is a fluid affair; with literally nothing to grasp, the emphasis is on texture and play, with all exploratory actions infinitely reversible.

As an empire of signs, Japan is the self-apparently systematic country in which Barthes finds himself at home. Within literature the writers he feels most comfortable reading are in similar ways builders of their own obvious systems, and in *Sade/Fourier/Loyola* he takes three figures not usually grouped together and finds that each constructs his own language perfectly suited to the codes he wishes to employ. What interests Barthes is Sade's "scriptural aspect": the activity of a man whose writing constructs novelistic structures which are also erotic structures, the rhetoric of which yields a novelistic flow "into which we are plunged" (*GV*, pp. 253–54). All three writers fabricate a language, taking semantic units (sexual variations, phalansteries of utopian order, stages of meditation and prayer) and establishing a syntax by which these units combine. "Sade, Fourier, and Loyola," Barthes shows, "write in terms of their desire. And they produce languages according to their desire, languages of desire" (*GV*, p. 257).

Sade's language is the most aggressive, as sperm is made the substitute for speech, described in the terms used for oratory. His erotic code follows the logic of the language which constitutes it, developed and extended infinitely according to its own rhetoric. Sade's very outrageousness as an author is built into his method, and his crimes can only be measured by the magnitude of the language devoted to them, for language alone can construct them. He can be criticized on moral grounds only when that standard exists outside of his own discourse; once we as readers enter it, we are his. "The impossibilities of the referent are turned into the possibilities of the discourse" (*SFL*, p. 36), and as the maker of his language Sade always favors discourse over reference, semiosis over mimesis. His discourse is founded on its own repetitions, and even this act is linguistic in character. Every part of the body is saturated by his eroticism; each part functions in his grammar. Like a sentence, the body has all of its sites filled by an expansion of possibilities. There is no structural reason why anything must terminate: the generation of sentences and erotic events is limitless. There is also no satisfaction, because there is no certainty of completion, a fact which in the sentence distressed Flaubert but in the erotics of the body delighted Sade. Combinations can never be exhausted; desire can never be fulfilled.

Sade's world occupies the space of language, and language-making activities fill it according to eminently linguistic practices. With Fourier we see an even more elemental process, that of "the signifier in action" (*SFL*, p. 87), reducing all unities to the single principle of Passion, "the absolute grapheme of the utopian text" (*SFL*, p. 100). Everything grows syntactically from this root. In similar manner Loyola sees every act as paradigmatic, and so constructs a language of meditation in which abstract things find their material movement, seeking a foundation of meaning on matter rather than on concept. In Loyola's text, "Semiologically, the image always sweeps on beyond the signified toward the pure materiality of the referent" (*SLF*, p. 62), a veritable language tree which leads one to the materiality of the Cross, which in turn validates the language growing from it. This circumstance does not strike Barthes as extreme or bizarre. Quite the contrary, for "There is no place without language" (*GV*, p. 162); nothing is real without it, since it is the very image of "a structured and decentered ensemble" (*GV*, p. 170), whose meaning resides not in a signified kernel of hidden truth but in the organizational mechanics of its signifying.

The dictionary is one such source of decentered structuration, and Barthes finds it a useful metaphor for what is new in his method: not structuring, but doing so without the influence (and prejudice) of a center of meaning. Although this practice is quintessentially postmodern, the capability has always been present in discourse, and Barthes is adept at showing its range of forms. The maxim is a common one, thanks to its practice of signifying by the syntactic device of antithesis. Structure and not rhetoric is the key, for more than a decorum of thought antithesis is a way of producing meaning from opposition, a fundamental procedure of signification; as a mechanism, it is devoid of meaning in itself.

Thus a maxim can present not a gradual flow of thought but its complete substance, thanks to this decentered structuring device which yields "a veritable *metrical* economy of thought" as each element has its requisite strong or weak beat filling out a fixed, finite space (*NCE*, p. 6). This is how language finds meaning according to its own structure, absorbing relationships within it by giving preference to the stronger metrical beats. Flaubert's emphasis of style takes advantage of just such structures; his "corrections of style" affect not the rhetoric of his content but rather "the primary code, that of the language; they commit the writer to experiencing the structure of the language as a passion" (*NCE*, p. 71). In this manner style engages the writer's full existence, since its reference is to his or her other writing (on the page, where the axes of the paper are the same as of language) and not to a realm of conceptualized meaning; as Flaubert says, writing the book is his way of living. Barthes sees writing the same way, and defends it as such against Raymond Picard's accusation that his critical method is simply an indulgence in jargon:

> Je défends ici le droit au langage, non mon propre "jargon." Comment pourrais-je d'ailleurs en parler? Il y a un profond malaise (un malaise d'identité) à imaginer que l'on puisse être propriétaire d'une certaine parole, et qu'il soit nécessaire de la défendre comme un bien dans ses caractères d'être. Suis-je donc *avant* mon langage? Qui serait ce *je,* propriétaire de ce qui précisément le fait être? Comment puis-je vivre mon langage comme un simple attribut de ma personne? Comment croire que si je parle, c'est parce que je suis? Hors la littérature, il est peut-être possible d'entretenir ces illusions; mais la littérature est précisément ce qui ne le permet pas. (*CV,* p. 34)
>
> I defend here the right to language, not my own "jargon." How could I speak any other way? There is a profound uneasiness (uneasiness of identity) to image that one can be the owner of a certain way of speaking, and that it is necessary to defend it as part of one's being. Do I therefore exist *before* my language? Who would be this "I," the owner of that which precisely causes him to exist? How can I live my language as a simple attribute of my person? How to believe that if I speak, it is because I am? Outside of literature, it is perhaps possible to entertain these illusions; but literature is precisely that which does not permit it.

Therefore when we turn from the author to his or her work, we see that the sentence is, as Flaubert described it, a unit of life, a double reflection: "it is on the level of fabrication of sentences that the writer has created the history of this work" (*NCE,* p. 76).

The decentered meaning of structure is easy enough to recognize in the maxim and possible to determine within the style of a master such as Flaubert. But Barthes's goal is to locate this quality in all discourse, to discover the semiotics of the text in the realm of relationships he calls *signifiance.* This is the signifier in action, independent of its relation to objects of reference. It often escapes language's ability to comment; using film as an example, Barthes calls it the quality of the *filmic* which cannot be represented or described. *Signifiance* seeks texts not in their meaning but in their difference; "it tries to say no longer *from where* the text comes (historical criticism), nor even *how* it is made (structural analysis), but how it is unmade, how it explodes, disseminates—by what coded paths it *goes off*" (*IMT*, pp. 126–27). Style is an indication, sketching the "reign of the signifier" (*RB*, p. 76), just as the word itself "transports me because of the notion that *I am going to do something with it:* it is the thrill of a future praxis, something like an *appetite.* This desire makes the entire motionless chart of language vibrate" (*RB*, p. 129). Barthes's metaphors are apt, for *signifiance* is indeed a locus of activity, the quality of language which corresponds to the Action painter's activation of his or her materials. "If I were a painter," Barthes confesses, "I should paint only colors" (*RB*, p. 143).

Self-conscious exercises of style highlight the artifice of discourse. Certain structural techniques, such as antithesis, place this artifice in higher profile. But other devices are just as effective at lowering that profile, and among them Barthes makes a special complaint about *analogy.* Analogy implies an effect of nature, and discourages forms being seen as themselves. This disposition toward resemblances is a "captivating bait" (*RB*, p. 44) on which the bourgeois economy of "quantitative representation" (*OR*, p. 142) feeds. In drama this happens when the actor overarticulates, doing the audience's thinking for it; doing so violates Barthes's sense of structural unity, for "the excessive significance of the detail destroys the natural significance of the whole" (*OR*, p. 143). But bourgeois theatre delights in the spectacle of the actor addressing no one but Meaning itself, with the result that the actors seem as if they are struggling not with themselves or with their situation but with "a kind of obscure language, as if [their] only task were to make it somewhat intelligible" (*OR*, p. 144). This style of theatre fails because it becomes less a manifestation of relationships than a frantic attempt at translation. Here lies the fraudulent disjunction between signifier and signified, by which the object "no longer has an essence but takes refuge entirely within its attributes" (*CE*, p. 6), specifically those of the ruling class. Such codes are usually derived from books, but via their enforcements of power they turn culture into nature and therefore "appear to establish reality, 'Life'" (*SZ*, p. 206).

Barthes employs this same definition for his book *Mythologies:* myth "transforms history into nature," and does so not by lying or by staging a confession but by the more effective means of "inflection"

(*M*, p. 129). This inflection causes it to be read as a factual system, when in truth it is semiological; contingency is made to appear eternal, naturalizing what is in fact a transient bourgeois ideology. Forming an image to which time supplies a natural cast is accomplished by effacing any sense of history. Therefore myth is depoliticized speech, which in its passage from history to nature oversimplifies human acts to make them appear as essences: "it does away with all dialectics, with any going back beyond what is immediately visible, it organizes a world which is without contradictions because it is without depth, a world wide open and wallowing in the evident, it establishes a blissful clarity: things appear to mean something by themselves" (*M*, p. 143).

Such a world is profoundly uninteresting, but Barthes uncovers a great drama in showing how this bourgeois economy establishes itself. He confesses that his starting point for the essays collected as *Mythologies* and *The Eiffel Tower* was "a feeling of impatience at the sight of the 'naturalness' with which newspapers, art, and common sense constantly dress up a reality which, even though it is the one we live in, is undoubtedly determined by history" (*M*, p. 11). Uncovering this process makes Barthes something of an investigative reporter, exposing the "reprehensible and deceitful" confusion of a sign with what is signified (*M*, p. 28), since this is the practice by which the bourgeois power naturalizes its interpretation of the world. The sickness Barthes locates is the "disease of thinking in essences" (*M*, p. 75), a practice which immobilizes the world by creating a universal order which stratifies and fixes the hierarchy of bourgeois possessions. This "prohibition for man against inventing himself" (*M*, p. 155) enforces an unliveable reality, such as the "big wedding" of the bourgeoisie which through news and literature is enforced as the norm dreamed (if not lived) by the petit-bourgeois couple who in truth cannot bear its expense. By such an imposition "The bourgeoisie is constantly absorbing into its ideology a whole section of humanity which does not have its basic status and cannot live up to it except in imagination" (*M*, p. 141), and that imagination has already been effectively channeled and hence closed down. Exposing it makes Barthes not just a semiological analyst but a social reformer, and the appeal of his project is demonstrated by the fact that the essays of *Mythologies* and *The Eiffel Tower* were first written for and published at monthly intervals in such popular journals as *France-Observateur* and *Les Lettres nouvelles*.

Barthes's own program for a purification of language involves a return to a theory of the text that proscribes writing as a pure function of communication, the elucidation of which again prompts a habit of thought identifiable with Harold Rosenberg's:

> writing ... appears, then, as the very *surplus* of its own function; the painter helps us to understand that writing's truth is neither in its messages nor in the system of transmission which it constitutes for current meaning, still less in the psychological expressivity attributed to it as a suspect science, graphology, comprised by certain technocratic interests (expertise, tests), but in the hand which presses down and traces a line, i.e., in *the body which throbs* (which takes pleasure). (*RF*, p. 154)

Continuing his metaphor, Barthes explains that in painting color is not a background against which certain marks stand out but is rather the entire space within which the work pulses; looking at Oriental writing, the Occidental viewer rejects its ideogramic nature in an attempt to substitute speech for gesture, the very propensity for which allows the bourgeois economy to willfully confuse the temporal with the eternal, the particular with the universal. Writing as opposed to speech prevents such confusion, because whereas speech "always *appears* symbolical, introverted, ostensibly turned toward an occult side of language," writing is "nothing but a flow of empty signs, the movement of which is alone significant." By no means simply an "open route" through which the intentionality of speech passes, writing is "a hardened language which is self-contained and is in no way meant to deliver to its own duration a mobile series of approximations" (*WDZ*, p. 19). Speech is characterized as an expendability of words—words spent in the establishment of a bourgeois economy of meaning—but the firmness of writing only highlights such investment in ulterior concepts and motives.

Writing's independence from articulated reference does, however, allow it to be seized intact. Many of the essays collected for American readers in *The Eiffel Tower* (having been omitted from the earlier translation of *Mythologies* because of their proximity to parochially French affairs) reveal how the government undertakes such operations. "African Grammar," describing the language used to qualify France's relations with its colonies seeking independence, shows how a "purely axiomatic" vocabulary can be constructed on the very principle of writing having no value as communication and therefore constituting a language "intended to bring about a coincidence between norms and facts, and to give a cynical reality the guarantee of a noble reality" (*ET*, p. 103). This is accomplished by using language as a written code—as a code to itself, in which words are unrelated to content. Barthes sifts through the government's statements on Algeria and other African trouble spots and assembles a lexicon of deception, all possible because writing is its own system, here reflective not at all of reality but rather decipherable as the foreign office's own propagandistic construction. *Band*, for example, is the term used to describe a group of rebels; when a group of French must be named, the term *community* proves more amenable, just as during America's war in Vietnam enemy forces were grouped under the rubric of monolithic political affiliation ("Communist") while friendly troops were named by their nationalities. The hostilities are described in terms of cruelty and pain, so that the "state of war is masked under the noble garment of tragedy, as if the conflict itself were essentially Evil, and not a (remediable) evil. Colonization evaporates, engulfed in the halo of an impotent lament, which *recognizes* the misfortune in order to establish it only the more successfully" (*ET*, pp. 103–104). *Honor* becomes a *mana* word filling the empty gap between signifier and signified where there in fact exists a fully inadmissible meaning, that of colonial oppression. In similar manner *Destiny* is the term used to explain the process by which Algeria's fortunes have been joined to those of France; military conquest is never mentioned. Barthes anticipates the lexicon of Vietnam when he shows how governmental writing can reverse meanings 180 degrees, as when *pacification* becomes the new word for *war* (*ET*, p. 105).

The government's African grammar is delusory, but it is still a grammar, and Barthes invokes the necessity of his analytical role by deconstructing its operations:

> The predominance of substantives in the whole vocabulary, of which we have just provided a few samples, derives obviously from the huge consumption of concepts necessary to the cover-up of reality. Though general and advanced to the last degree of decomposition, the exhaustion of this language does not attack verbs and substantives in the same way: it destroys the verb and inflates

the noun. Here moral inflation bears on neither objects nor actions, but always on ideas, "notions," whose assemblage obeys less a communication purpose than the necessity of a petrified code. Codification of the official language and its substantivation thus go hand in hand, for the myth is fundamentally nominal, insofar as nomination is the first procedure of distraction. (*ET,* p. 107)

Grammatically, the verb attains meaning only in the future, where it is less likely to be contradicted. And so what is in fact a subjective view on the part of the government is encoded as an account of reality. The persuasiveness of that account depends upon how well the writing is handled, which is certainly a literary quality, and which brings us full circle to Barthes's account of what literature is, namely "that ensemble of objects and rules, techniques and works, whose function in the general economy of our society is precisely *to institutionalize subjectivity*" (*OR,* p. 172).

Is all writing thus a persuasion? Barthes answers yes, but makes an important distinction: that "whenever it's the *body* which writes, and not ideology, there's a chance the text will join us in our modernity" (*GV,* p. 191). *Modernité* is the French term used for "postmodernism," and Barthes's linkage of it to "the body" marks an important aspect of his thought. In *A Lover's Discourse* he describes song as "the precious addition to a blank message, entirely contained within its address, for what I give by singing is at once my body (by my voice) and the silence into which you cast that body" (*LD,* p. 77). Barthes draws a running comparison between music and writing in the muscularity of their exercise: both writer and singer are able to experience the materiality of their text as it passes through their fingers, either at the desk or piano. The fact that Michelet "really introduced the body into history," rethinking it through "its suffering, its humors, blood, physiologies, and foods" (*GV,* p. 337), makes him one of Barthes's favorite authors, and it is a sense of his own body that places Barthes in history: "I can push my body to its own limits only with an Other, but this other also has a body, an image-repertoire" (*GV,* p. 365) whose materiality reminds the author of his own.

Barthes's sense of body must be studied with his notion of abstraction, for it is abstract relationships which signify. In *The Fashion Sys-*

tem he continually reminds us that the relationship between clothes and their styles or occasions are syntagmatic, that it is "the abstract nature of this connection which produces meaning, not the materiality of the elements associated" (*FS*, p. 153). The principle supporting the nature of system is difference, but not of simple binary opposition; yet it is the opposition which signifies, and not the thing in itself, and that opposition is sustained by a syntax which unites the signifying units. Meaning derives from variation, and that variation depends upon the degree of freedom syntagmatic association allows. Hence the "rotation of the forms of Fashion" which is "never concerned with anything but the terms of the variant and not with the variants themselves" (*FS*, p. 179), forming the cradle of Barthes's abstraction. The effectiveness of this abstraction will be measured by its power of constraint, and that is why the fashion system is so interesting. If a thick wool sweater is to be made fashionable by the connotations of an autumn weekend in the country, the directive must succeed through the persuasiveness of its connection, for there is no coded correspondence between the sweater and the season in the country; the correspondence is manufactured by the systematic relationship, which is free to change (and undoubtedly will in next year's styles). Syntax is only a combination, but a combination which constrains for a time and then retreats.

Only reading can bring life to a syntactic arrangement, and in this practice Barthes brings the materiality of writing into play. His clearest example of this act is in his analysis of the Eiffel Tower as a vehicle for reading. One goes to the Tower not to see it but to see Paris, and from its vantage point the city becomes particularly readable—not just perceived, but ordered in a way which "permits us to transcend sensation and to see things *in their structure*" (*ET*, p. 9). Separate points are distinguished yet remain linked, their places deciphered within a new space. This is what intelligence is, the ability "to *reconstitute,* to make memory and sensation cooperate so as to produce in your mind a similacrum of Paris, of which the elements are in front of you, real, ancestral, but nonetheless disoriented by the total space in which they are given to you, for this space was unknown to you" (*ET,* p. 10). And so even though the syntactic arrangement of Paris is abstract, its reading is a physical, corporeal affair, an act which depends upon the viewer's physical placement in the Tower. For writing to be seen the same way, to the extent that it "absorbs the whole identity of a literary work"

(*WDZ*, p. 85), it must possess the same physical voice as that which reads it. Writer and reader meet in the physical presence of this act, "not in its syntagmatic extension, but in its raw and as though vertical *signifying*" (*RF*, p. 259) where by deconstructing itself reading is externalized, giving up its inwardness to meet the body of the text. Here one meets "the grain of the voice," which as in singing is "the materiality of the body speaking its mother tongue" (*RF*, p. 270). When writing moves us, it is because something has been moved in the chain of the signifier; contrasts do not speak by themselves, but rather move to fulfill a certain radiancy in the writing itself, a process which does not "follow" but rather "explodes" (*RF*, p. 302).

For this meeting to take place, the text must be conceived of as a production, just as Harold Rosenberg envisioned the work of art. And as Rosenberg introduces the concept of action to replace representation, Barthes replaces signification with *signifiance*. This emphasis on production casts off the legal, monological status of the former term, and draws new attention to the "mobile play of signifiers, with no possible reference to one or several fixed signifieds" (*UT*, p. 37). Signification is something which happens on the level of product, but the signifying work of *signifiance* happens in the realm of production. The language of writing enters the reader in order to work him or her and undo previous senses of signification—*signifiance* is therefore the text actively at work within the reader. It is "the glow, the unpredictable flash of the infinities of language" (*UT*, p. 40), a quality Rosenberg can apply to painting as well; for both, an intertextual resonance is more important than any simply lawful meaning. Avenues of meaning are sought, rather than the terminus of any one meaning.

Barthes's linkage of the singing voice with writing is interesting, for it shows the importance he accords the voice as the "privileged (eidetic) site of difference" (*RF*, p. 279) and song as "the field [*champ* or *chant*] of celebration" of language (*RF*, p. 281). Painting can in similar manner be appreciated in terms of breath, especially when Cy Twombly's works use aerated spaces to convey such an energy which makes it "easier to breathe" (*RF*, p. 182), the same sense of physical, living body which Rosenberg finds in Action Painting. Hand and not eye is the essence of painting for both critics, and when Barthes turns to music the basis of his aesthetic remains the same: "The music you play depends not so much on an auditive as on a manual (hence much more sensuous) activity" in which the body listens, not the soul—"the body itself must transcribe what it reads: it fabricates sound and sense: it is the scriptor, not the receiver; the decoder" (*RF*, p. 261). The "grain" Barthes so treasures is "the body in the singing voice, in the writing hand, in the performing limb" (*RF*, p. 276), and in all cases this grain emerges from the friction caused between what it is and what it is not. This savoring of the grain is most apparent in the performance of the amateur, *"the one who does not exhibit"* (*RF*, p. 230), but who handles the work for pure enjoyment, an act which by insulating the self from professed meaning highlights the pleasure of the work itself:

> The enormous benefit of the amateur's situation is that it involves no image-repertoire, no narcissism. When one draws or paints as an amateur, there is no preoccupation with the *imago*, the image one will project of oneself in making the drawing or painting. It's thus a liberation, I would almost say a liberation from civilization. To be included in a utopia à la Fourier. A civilization where people would act without being preoccupied with the image of themselves they will project to others. (*GV*, pp. 216–17)

How the reader produces this text by vitalizing its cultural codes is given full study in *S/Z*. Barthes's reading of the Balzac novella *Sarrasine* is itself a physical expansion, as it takes 214 pages to reproduce the action of Balzac's 33-page text. But the operation of reading is also a physical reduction, for the tale's many sentences (and even more detailed actions) are reduced to 561 *lexias* which Barthes sees as the units of reading (just as a morpheme is the smallest divisible unit of linguistic meaning). This relative physical expansion and contraction is not strictly analytical, since it reproduces rather than disassembles the writer's act in constructing *Sarrasine*. Unlike the classical rhetoricians, Barthes has no interest in constructing the text, which would involve reorganizing it into much larger masses of meaning. Instead, he prefers to let each unit signify completely, limited only by the cultural codes of its writing—and as a result the final ensemble exists only once all the codes are in place and functioning, rather than letting a preconceived terminal meaning shape an understanding of those codes.

"The more plural the text, the less it is written before I read it" (*SZ*, p. 10)—with this, Barthes announces his goal in reading, which is to reenact the writing of the text itself, just as Harold Rosenberg's art audience reenacts the painting of an Action canvas. In this manner even rereading is more play than consumption, since everything is allowed to signify without limit until the accumulation of codes assumes its direction toward the text's total effect. "Writerly value," as Barthes puts it, transforms the reader from consumer to producer, and in so doing activates the text itself, just as Action Painting is kept alive by viewing. "The writerly text is a perpetual present," Barthes explains, "upon which no *consequent* language (which would inevitably make it past) can be superimposed; the writerly text is *ourselves writing,* before the infinite play of the world (the world as function) is traversed, intersected, stopped, plasticized by some singular system (Ideology, Genus, Criticism) which reduces the plurality of entrances, the opening of networks, the infinity of languages" (SZ, p. 5). It is at once apparent that Barthes's new method avoids the restrictive meaning of conventional criticism, for there is no way that his reading can be less than that of the full text itself. Yet the text is still made manageable; indeed, this sense of handling which allows the work's replay becomes a performance with finesse, for with each code understood the text is allowed its fullest meaning.

"To end, to fill, to join, to unify—one can say that this is the basic requirement of the *readerly*" (SZ, p. 105), and its one great fear is that of missing a connection. Note the process: the meaning lies in the abstraction known as syntax, in the connection of various elements according to cultural and linguistic codes; but for those connections to operate, the elements themselves must be vitalized by the act of reading, and this involves the action of the *writerly* text. The text can express the reader's interest, a displaced voice by which the discourse speaks according to the reader's interests. This is why in the text only the reader speaks, for the individual elements mean nothing by themselves but everything *when combined,* and it is the reader who enacts that combination, making it happen in his or her action. Here Barthes finds true readerly value, the ability to fill in the chains of causality. The network of codes Barthes establishes creates a topology through which the full text passes, which is not a structure the reader discovers but rather a structuration the reading will produce. The meaning of a text lies not in an interpretation, which may vary from critic to critic and therefore never be complete, but in a diagrammatic totality of readings—a plural system. A single meaning, after all, is a force which seeks to dominate other forces, other meanings, and the strongest of all will be that whose systematization includes the largest number of elements. There is room for narrative development in Barthes's vision of the text, for sequences are "the positions held and then left behind in the course of a gradual invasion of meaning" (*SZ*, p. 160). The virtue of his method is that no position is excluded from a reading, since the enactment of writerly process guarantees each element its due in the work's structuration.

The authority of the text, therefore, rests ultimately in its reading, but only when this reading completely reenacts the process of its writing. In this way Barthes keeps the text intact while radicalizing its sense of operation, just as Rosenberg does for painting. Writing gives to the imaginary "the formal guarantee of the real" (*WDZ*, p. 33), and Barthes is always suspicious of the narrative's pretense of authority, from its use of the preterite (behind which "there always lurks a demiurge, a God or reciter") to its para-historical expression of an order, "and consequently of a euphoria" (*WDZ*, pp. 30–31). The mythical "he" of the traditional novel's third-person narration is much like the preterite tense in that it gives readers a sense of security "born of a credible fabrication which is yet constantly held up as false" (*WDZ*, p. 35), for the "he" of each novel's syntactic arrangements operates in perfectly grammatical order yet never really exists. Literature has found several ways to make texts convey meaning more directly. In *Writing Degree Zero*, before Robbe-Grillet's work is available in any great extent for analysis, Barthes singles out the "neutral style" of Camus which emulates a "transparent form of speech," reducing writing to "a sort of negative mood in which the social or mythical characters of a language are abolished in favor of a neutral and inert state of form" in which thought can be responsible for itself "without being overlaid by a secondary commitment of form to a History not its own" (*WDZ*, p. 77). In *Mythologies* he identifies contemporary poetry (that which does not impose the "extra signified" of metrical regularity) as a "regressive semiological system" which instead of amplifying a system (like myth) "attempts to regain an infra-signification, a pre-semiological state of language: in short, it tries to transform the sign back into meaning" (*M*, p. 133), reaching not the meaning of words but of things themselves. Poetry is therefore the opposite of myth, for instead of being a semiological system which pretends to transcend itself into the realm of fact, it tries instead to contract itself into the world of essences. But mankind's practical existence makes such essentiality impossible, for as an object is used, that very use tends to "dissipate its essential form and emphasize instead its attributes" (*CE*, p. 5). Mankind never confronts the object directly, but rather its subjugated practicality—in other words, not what it is but rather what it can do for the person, which is an assigned value rather than a natural one. In the artifice of that assignment begins the whole writerly and readerly project which eventually leads to the text.

Therefore Barthes urges us to look not at the signification of a thing, but at its function within the signifier, "of the thing which has been robbed" (*M*, p. 145). Otherwise we are held prisoner to the dogma of myth, which moves beyond the instrumental grasp of the world as object to the second-level metalanguage of bourgeois aphorism "which bears on objects already prepared," transforming historical products into essential types. Within this metalanguage there is no freedom:

> For the very end of myths is to immobilize the world: they must suggest and mimic a universal order which has fixated once and for all the hierarchy of possessions. Thus, every day and everywhere, man is stopped by myths, referred by them to this motionless prototype which lives in his place, stifles him in the manner of a huge internal parasite and assigns to his activity the narrow limits within which he is allowed to suffer without upsetting the world: bourgeois pseudo-physics is in the fullest sense a prohibition for man against inventing himself. (*M*, p. 155)

Thus is accomplished the great bourgeois task of reducing a being to a thing, establishing an economy in which reality "is not even what is seen, it is what is counted" (*ET*, p. 52).

The text should be a codified expression of the Other, but again and again Barthes shows how the petit-bourgeois person is unable to imagine it. The Other remains the unknown, essentially unknowable because such is the state that is wished: during the Cold War of Iron Curtain politics, the Soviet Union assumes for Westerners "the very otherness of a planet" (*ET*, p. 27) to the extent that popular mythology can suggest extraterrestrial flying saucers may indeed come from the USSR. On the other hand, what is truly the Other, such as the uninvestigated planet Mars, is "implicitly endowed with a historical determinism copied from that of Earth," so that it becomes "merely an imagined Earth, endowed with perfect wings, as in all dreams of idealization" (*ET*, p. 28). A sign can mean anything, from which knowledge, history, and dreams can be extracted. This is how myths are made, as meanings are created.

Once signs are invested with meaning, they become signals of value where none exist: *The Eiffel Tower* is filled with such examples, from the practice that an actor does not exist until his or her publicity photo has been prepared in a certain manner by a specific studio, to the music hall gestures of evangelist Billy Graham, whose pressure of delivery, break of logical links, verbal repetitions, and "the grandiloquent designation of the Bible held at arm's length like the universal can opener of a quack peddler" (*ET*, p. 65) all combine to form the play of signs in place of any solid reality. When a narrative action does occur, as in the Tour de France, Barthes notes that the popular imagination can absorb it only once the riders have been invested with mythical qualities, making the Tour "an uncertain conflict of certain essences" (*ET*, p. 87).

Cold War politics of the unknowable date from Barthes's first emergence as a writer. But in the mid-1970s, when his own work was well in hand, another potentially alien phenomenon presented itself: China, a land where a political overthrow followed by a cultural revolution had closed the doors to visitors for nearly thirty years. Barthes approaches this China with thousands of questions, from sexuality, women, and the family to the new culture's human sciences, linguistics, and psychiatry. Yet his eagerness of inquiry does not yield answers:

> Nous agitons l'arbre du savior pour que la réponse tombe et que nous puissions revenir pourvus de ce qui est notre principale nourriture intellectuelle: un secret déchiffré. Mais rien ne tombe. En un sens, nous revenons (hors la réponse politique) avec: *rien*. (*AC*, p. 7)

> We shake the tree of knowledge to make an answer fall, and to provide ourselves again with our chief intellectual nourishment: a decoded secret. But nothing falls. In a sense, we return (excepting the political answer) with: *nothing*.

This nothing, however, is not a vacancy that exists on the part of the Chinese, for Barthes soon discovers that he has been interrogating not them but himself. They seem to resist his reading not through deception, but because his very forms of concepts, themes, and even names have been undone in their process of exchange: "elle ne partage pas les cibles du savior comme nous; le champ sémantique est désorganisé" (*AC*, p. 8: "they do not share the targets of knowledge with us; the semantic field is disorganized"). Because Barthes poses his questions without thought of this difference, the answers are returned in kind, making knowledge a fantasy and allowing silence to be considered impertinent. This is the end of interpretation, Barthes declares, and signals the blank standoff in China's relations with the West.

With the essence of China left unknowable, Barthes finds that we are given instead tactful samples and platitudes: ancient palaces, children's ballet, and Chairman Mao himself. As a result, the China we know lacks dimensions—it is not "colored" in the sense Barthes requires for the understanding of a culture. Individual pieces of information might be known, but when the field of knowledge fades into a flat uniformity, unshaded by nuances of meaning, the semiologist is unable to do his work. Japan, where Barthes can organize and appreciate codes, has been known to the West since the mid-sixteenth century, but contemporary China still hides behind our ignorance.

What perplexes Barthes is the apparent uniformity of gesture and dress, a state of affairs which invites (to Western eyes) a feeling of boredom or derision, simply because these materials cannot be seen as taking part in any process of signification—and by the same terms, offering no possibilities for the erotic or the dramatic. Instead, the most appropriate word which comes to Barthes's mind is *paisible* (*AC*, p. 10: "peaceful"), because there is none of the agitation evident which characterizes the making of meaning. *Significance*, we recall, is for Barthes the moving play of signifiers quite apart from the level on which meaning is produced; but without knowing which are the meanings, there is no chance to identify that realm of play apart from meaning, which is where the erotics of the text may be found. Western audiences are not privileged to see Chinese semantics in action, except for politics, which is the only text we are given to read:

> Ce Texte est partout: aucun domaine ne lui est soustrait: dans tous les discours que nous avons entendus, la Nature (le naturel, l'éternel) ne parle plus (sauf sur un point, curieusement résistant:

la famille, épargnée, semble-t-il, par la critique menée actuellement contre Confucius). (AC, pp. 10–11)

This text is everywhere: no area escapes it; in all of the discourse which we have heard, Nature (the natural, the eternal) no longer speaks (except on one point, curiously resistant: the family, which is saved, it seems, by criticism actually directed at Confucius).

Because this political frame of reference shapes every assertion, Barthes realizes that China is beyond his ability to comment. He appreciates it simply as one listens to music, without judging its truth or falsity. China's overtly political language of epic struggle subsumes our own semantic distinctions, leaving no room for the action of a writer who wishes to interpret in semiological terms.

Barthes's talents are better exercised in the realm of *writing,* free from the implied transcendent status of both "politics" and "literature." Notice how he distances himself from the latter term, so that his own activity of reading is given more prominent play:

> Pour moi, la littérature—je parle toujours, évidemment, d'une littérature en quelque sorte exemplaire, exemplairement subversive, et c'est pourquoi j'aimerais mieux l'appeler *écriture*—est toujours une perversion, c'est-à-dire une pratique qui vise à ébranler le sujet, à le dissoudre, à le disperser à même la page. Pendant très longtemps, parce que l'idéologie de l'époque était une idéologie de la représentation, de la figuration, cela s'est produit dans les oeuvres classiques d'une façon détournée; mais en réalité, il y avait dèja à ce moment-là de l'écriture, c'est-à-dire de la perversion. (SL, pp. 16–17)

For me, literature—I always speak, obviously, of a literature in some way exemplary, exemplarily subversive, and that is why I would rather call it *writing*—is always a perversion, in other words a practice which aims to weaken the subject, to dissolve it, to disperse it even on the page. For a very long time, because the ideology of the times was an ideology of representation, of figuration, this was produced in classical works in a roundabout fashion; but in reality it had existed before that moment of writing, that is to say of perversion.

Barthes's example is the novel *Bouvard et Pécuchet,* a work which condenses all these problems by dramatizing the affairs of two copyists in a carousel of imitated language. Because languages imitate each other, there is no end to language, just as there is no spontaneous origin to it—just a perpetual crossing of codes whose source is never found. For Barthes, literature itself is much like this example from Flaubert.

This free play of language is an activity Barthes defends against all challenges. His *Critique et Vérité* is a response to Raymond Picard's complaint that the *nouvelle critique* which *On Racine* employs is really a *nouvelle imposture* (new fraudulence) based on subjectivity and psychoanalysis of the dead. Barthes replies that what Picard describes as concrete objectivity is simply "the habitual," and that it is the habitual which determines the taste of verisimilitude; the supposedly realist critic, therefore, is citing neither objects nor ideas, "mais seulement de valeurs" (*CV*, p. 24: "but only values"). Taste, Barthes insists, is an interdiction of the free play of language, in Picard's case cutting off the erotic from the intellectual. As a result, just one more jargon is created, the so-called "clarté française" (French clarity) being just one cast of mind among others. But whereas bourgeois society has seen language as an instrument of decoration, Barthes employs it in the double-edged game of signification and *signifiance,* enhancing its role within the human imagination.

Hence when Barthes proposes a method to counter Picard's charges of fraud, it is a system based not on content but on the conditions which can generate it—not just a history of literature, but a science. Once one admits that literature is made, such a science becomes practical, for the matter of study will be the possible variations ("polyvalence," *CV*, p. 57) and not just the product of symbolization. Just as there is a faculty of language, there can be a faculty of literature, capable of generating certain forms of works, and such a perspective avoids the pitfalls of taste and implied value. But it is to this point that traditional critics object, since "For science, language is merely an instrument, which it chooses to make as transparent, as neutral as possible, subjugated to scientific matters (operations, hypotheses, results) which are said to exist outside it and to precede it" (*RL*, p. 4). It then becomes the critic's job to show how from this neutral language derives any number of literary uses—poetry, fiction, and so forth—which operate according to their own codes, and chief among these will be the codes of pleasure.

Thus when Barthes proposes a reading as he does of *Sarrasine*, he does not reconstitute *a* reader but rather *the* reader, who is conducted through the codes of languages inherited from uncountable narratives through the ages which form the reader's birthright. And because this birthright is held in common, subjectivity is not a cause for worry. Instead, the reader's inheritance of literary codes unites him or her with the writer, the perfect union of which constitutes Barthes's ideal for literature which is much like Rosenberg's for painting:

> En fait, le grand problème, maintenant, c'est de faire du lecteur un écrivain. Le jour où l'on arrivera à faire du lecteur un écrivain virtuel ou potentiel, tous les problèmes de lisibilité disparaîtront. Si on lit un text apparemment illisible, dans le mouvement de son écriture, on le comprend très bien. Evidemment, toute une transformation,—je dirais presque une éducation—est à faire; pour cela, il faut une transformation sociale. De même qu'il y a eu en peinture l'*action-painting,* j'envisagerais bien quelque chose comme l'*action-writing,* mais à supposer, bien entendu, qu'il ait aussi des circuits nombreux pour ces textes, de façon à ce qu'on ne soit pas agressé par des textes "casse-pieds," si je puis dire, c'est-à-dire inadéquats. (*SL,* pp. 46–47).

> In fact, the big problem is now to make the reader a writer. When the day comes that the reader is made into a virtual or potential writer, all problems of readability will disappear. If one reads an apparently unreadable text, in the movement of its writing, one comprehends very well. Evidently a complete transformation—I should say almost an education—is needed; for that, one needs a social transformation. Just as there has been in painting *action painting,* I would forsee as well such a thing as *action writing,* but supposing of course that there would also be numerous channels for the text, so that one would not be attacked by "boring" texts, if I can say—that is, inadequate.

This utopia, Barthes insists, is a possible one, because the style of reading he envisions is a true erotics of the text. Once the text is seen as inscribed on the body of the reader, reading becomes an amorous rapport between two bodies corresponding not to individuals in the civil or moral sense but as figures formed by their discursive subjects.

The inscription of the text on the reader's body may sound like an exotic notion, but it is an overtly physical clue to Roland Barthes's method as a critic. When he looks for a sign system, it is not the abstract sense of that system that attracts him but rather its physical immediacy—hence his interest in the fashion system, because clothes not only possess an intellectual existence which is subject to systematic analysis by formal means but also possess a daily existence which gives him "an opportunity for self-knowledge on the most immediate level (since I invest myself in my own life)" (*GV*, p. 43). He admits that his happiest book is *S/Z* because the experience of writing it yielded "the blissful pleasure of work, and of writing" (*GV*, p. 69), a time in his life "when I felt the necessity of entering completely into the signifier" (*GV*, p. 84). Mankind is indeed the sign-making animal, and combining signs is the activity of this species' play: "At every moment of my life, wherever I go, even walking in the street, when I think, react, I constantly find myself on the side of thought that grapples with what is discontinuous and combinatory." This is indeed the nature of Barthes's physical and not just intellectual existence: "what I want, after all, is precisely to feel the juxtaposition of things, the 'next to'" (*GV*, p. 132).

The writer's body becomes known in this same way, not as a biography of the writer but of his or her oeuvre, a "kind of ergography" which Barthes explains in his own work as "the history of a game, a playful succession of texts that I have tried out: which is to say that I've tried out registers of different models, different fields of citation," from *The Fashion System,* which cites certain models combining to form a system, to *Empire of Signs,* which enters completely into the signifier to treat the *"writing"* itself (*GV*, pp. 145–46). His primary interest is in the seduction of the text—why does it seduce a writing, and then become a thing of desire to the reader? Desire itself is first vested in a graphic impulse, which in Barthes's case is his own calligraphy. But then "there is the critical moment when this object is prepared for the anonymous and collective consumption of others through transformation into a typographical object" (*GV*, p. 179), which anticipates the revitalization of the text through an erotics of reading.

"What I do within myself is philosophize, reflect on my experience"

(*GV*, p. 307)—this simple dedication, which Barthes characterizes as a pleasurable activity to be pursued, indicates that he makes of his own being an activity much like the Action Painting Harold Rosenberg describes and the action writing Barthes proposes. This activist mode of living engenders a particular quality which the essays and interviews from the last five years of his life cite with increasing frequency. "In daily life, I feel a sort of curiosity for everything I see and hear, almost an intellectual affectivity" which goes beyond even his semiotic habit of comparison and system-building to become something "on the order of the novelistic" (*GV*, p. 203). But unlike the nineteenth century's realistic novelist who would have strolled through life with notebook at ready, Barthes finds himself unable to take the historically obsolete step of composing a story with characters and anecdotal events; like Paul Valéry, he is unable to write something on the order of "the Marchioness went out at five o'clock," because such a statement implies an action which emerges "from a past without substance" and which "purged of the uncertainty of existence" has "the stability and outline of an algebra," a "recollection, the interest of which far surpasses its duration" (*WDZ*, p. 31). This suspension of disbelief is the Coleridgean doctrine Barthes most wishes to avoid, but his breakthrough is to realize that "I can write novelistically without ever writing novels" (*RF*, p. 59; *IMT*, p. 65).

"The novelistic is a mode of discourse unstructured by a story" (*GV*, p. 222), Barthes advises, coining a word which suggests the same sense as *painterly* has among the axioms of Harold Rosenberg's beliefs: a notion which preserves the artistic action as a self-reflective process rather than as a motive pledged to a final product. Barthes confesses that he would very much like to work with novelistic experiences and utterances, and in doing so has made his *Roland Barthes* less of a biography than a work which caresses the novelistic surfaces of life so that an image-repertoire can be staged—in other words, "the very discourse of the novel" (*GV*, p. 223). Because his vision is essentially fragmented, he finds himself moving progressively closer to the novel form itself (*GV*, p. 285), and admits that this disposition could easily make him "a structuralist today, a novelist tomorrow" (*GV*, p. 322). In music, he admires the Schubertian and Schumannian song because of its ability "at once to imagine and to improvise: in short, to hallucinate, this journey is in a sense turned back on itself, blind, closed to any general meaning, to any notion of fate, to any spiritual transcendence." What Barthes finds here is what he seeks in the life of his own works: "a pure *wandering*, a becoming without finality: at one stroke, and to infinity, to begin everything all over again" (*RF*, p. 291).

Four

Ihab Hassan

Re-visioning Man

We need first to understand that the human form—including human desire and all its external representations—may be changing radically, and thus must be re-visioned. We need to understand that five hundred years of humanism may be coming to an end, as humanism transforms itself into something that we must helplessly call posthumanism. The figure of Vitruvian Man, arms and legs defining the measure of things, so marvelously drawn by Leonardo, has broken through its enclosing circle and square, and spread across the cosmos (RPF, p. 201). In Ihab Hassan's suggestion we can trace the consequence of Harold Rosenberg's reformulation of painting and Roland Barthes's reshaping of the act of writing: with the painter redefined in relation to his or her act of painting, and the writer now identified as someone other than a poser of transparencies, an entirely new world seems to be at hand, the result of "some decisive historical mutation" bearing upon our notion of "the One and the Many" (*DO-II*, p. 271). As Rosenberg and Barthes do with the roles of painter and writer, Hassan compresses the critic's job into an essence of activity only to reshape our understanding of its larger nature. In studying this essence, we find that it calls for an enlargement of our sense of what the critic does; as with Action Painting and action writing, concentrating on the act in process widens the field rather than narrowing it. "This is not a time for professors of literature to ignore the judgments of human passions" (*RI*, p. 326), Hassan urges, and the literature he undertakes to criticize in his first work is seen not as a static point in history but as a vitalistic concern, as alive as his own act of engagement. "The contemporary American novel does not only aver our presence," he insists, "it explores and enlarges the modalities of our *being*" (*RI*, p. 3).

Like Rosenberg and Barthes, Hassan expands the implications of his critical method as he enlarges the nature of his subject. For him the novel is more than a report from society; it is a dialectic between self and world, a reality managed by the artist's constructions, and because of its extraordinary way of handling these matters the American novel becomes his initial subject, just as Rosenberg is drawn to Action Painting and Barthes to the making of writing systems: "The anarchy in the American soul is nourished on an old dream: not freedom, not power, not even love, but the dream of immortality. America has never really acknowledged Time. Its vision of Eden or Utopia is essentially a timeless vision. Its innocence is neither geographical nor moral: it is mainly temporal, hence metaphysical. This is a radical innocence" (*RI*, p. 325). The world invites initiation, but Hassan finds this initiation to be especially problematic in America's self-conception as a land of innocence and promise as against the record and restraints of European experience. When this initiation to innocence rather than experience reaches a state of crisis, particularly "a crisis of confidence in the 'American way of life'" (*CAL*, p. 3), the two literatures find a new affinity, to the extent that contemporary American fiction derives from Dostoevsky's *Notes from Underground* as well as from Twain's *Adventures of Huckleberry Finn*. Yet as these two examples suggest, the characteristic American fictive act remains a play on the surface, madly hopscotching from one crisis to another in the attempt to avoid being sucked into depth. "What continues to distinguish the American from the European novel is its critical awareness of *loss,* its ironic cultivation of human *vulnerability,* its bitter generosity toward all things *quixotic* and infrangible" (RI, p. 60). Yet this surface can be enjoyed naturally, with no need to hold compulsively to the materials of strict observation: there is no need for a nouveau roman in America.

Hassan's *The Literature of Silence* offers an apt contrast between the American and European manners, from Henry Miller's "voluble adventurers" scatting across the physical surface to Samuel Beckett's "taciturn mentalists" who permutate the world into logical nonexistence (LS, p. 210). Posed between these two worlds, Hassan himself notes the difference as he passes from Old to New: "Europe possesses a past; America makes one; but the past America makes becomes elsewhere in the world an optative future. That is, America, alembic of time, distills the future in the present, and so permits other nations to choose their destiny. This does not always win gratitude" (OE, pp. 45–46). The American novel is formed by this same paradox, that an independence of time means not just freedom from the past but an "escape from the present" (RI, p. 38) that in effect gives mankind literally nowhere to stand; for all of Henry Miller's riotous joy in the physically real, the life of his novel yields nothing to hold or to build on. More simply begets more; initiation is endless, with only the Self existing, "eternally poised on the eve of Creation. This is the song American literature sings" (RI, p. 326).

As a country without a prehistory, America suddenly finds itself within history "with the intention to rape and redeem time in its heart" (RI, p. 336), and from this especially "urgent sense of Being" (LS, p. 45) comes the Romantic sense of anarchy, self-reliance, and love which characterizes not just Henry Miller but Emerson, Thoreau, and Whitman. They do not fear history, but rather the corruption of their ahistorical dream. In their work time follows the rhythms of their emotions, not the demands of history, and Hassan fondly cites Blake's definition of America as "another portion of the infinite" (P, p. 176). This quality interests him for the same reasons Rosenberg hails the de-definition of art and Barthes appreciates the decentering impulse of semiotics: the historic lawlessness of the American experience "compounds itself with the current crisis of authority" (DD, p. 12) which contributes to a re-visioning of human nature. Yet this claim for a new vision implies something at once older than Europe or Egypt, "the precedence of a primeval jungle over the most archaic temple" (*OE*, p. 103). Hence the critic's formulation of a re-visioning rather than a reinventing. Postmodern thought is corrective and not simply transformational.

Much of the energy Hassan finds in contemporary American fiction is born of its opposition, and that opposition at first takes the form of irony. Yet irony is a limited mode, defined by its opposition rather than by what it hopes to be itself, and Hassan's investigations soon take him beyond the contemporary literary history *Radical Innocence* surveys. In this first work we find him faulting the novels of his time for suspending resolutions and beginning quests only to dissolve into plotlessness. What he sees in Salinger's late work is indicative of 1940s and 1950s fiction as a whole, that "the powers of spirit overreach the resources of form" (*RI*, p. 280) and that "Between the poles of silence and sentiment, language reels and totters" (*RI*, p. 264). It is for these same reasons that Barthes declines to write a novel in the conventional mode, and Hassan's vision as a critic grows faster than the literature around him. "Radical questions engage the total quality of our life," he announces at the start of *The Dismemberment of Orpheus;* "they are questions of being" which lead the critic to ponder whether the writer's imagination "may yet prove to be the teleological organ of evolution" (*DO*, p. ix).

Hassan asks if questions about human destiny belong in literary criticism, and answers that literature speculates about little else. He sees avant-garde writing inventing the future, and notes an experimental tendency toward vanishing forms, spinning free from history. The American Self which inspires Hassan's first work boasts an innocence that refuses to accept reality's rule and argues even against death, "an aboriginal Self the radical imperatives of whose freedom cannot be stifled" (*RI*, p. 6). There is indeed a great disparity between this hero's innocence and the destructive nature of his or her experience, but that is what creates the contemporary novel's energy and its promise of experiment. Reality may be a discovery of limits, but in Hassan's case it is of the limits we ourselves impose—which means a discovery of form. To exist, as in the works of Samuel Beckett, can be a case of watching oneself trying to exist, much as Sade "calls hell to the rescue, thinking thus to redeem the reality of fiction" from its perversions in Gothic sentiment and horror (*DO,* p. 43). Artaud, like Peter Handke in our own time, attacks not just the audience but its assumption of reality, especially a reality it presumes to possess. Hassan's favorite works reach out in a positive fashion, as does Bellow's *The Adventures of Augie March* which speaks for the possibilities of experience in an age when the Self finds it easier to withdraw into the pleasures of alienation. Bellow's reality is thus much larger than found in the work of other novelists, which reminds Hassan that anyone's sense of "what is really happening" is itself "a function of frames, which are a kind of fiction" (*RPF,* p. 3)—hence the infinite regressivity of narrative, yielding fictions of fictions. Frames create paradigms, which both enable and constrain. A truly generative effort of life transcends these frames at will, reconceiving reality and thus transforming the past as its paradigms are left behind. Logic itself must never be allowed to serve as a mode of dominion instead of agreement, nor become a conceptual ban. Logic is, after all, an abstract system, and the distinctions it breeds must remain dissolvable as they were first formable.

At issue in such contests is the question which Hassan asks in each of his critical books and prominently in his autobiography: "Can humanists learn to dream again, and dreaming wake to meditate actively between Culture and Desire, Language and Power, History and Hope?" (*OE,* p. 15). If indeed the modern experience has worked destructive forces upon the human form, leading to its critical breakdown, isn't the true hope to be found in our postmodern response? The causes for concern are manifest:

> History predicts no salvation for man and accords no meaning retrospectively to his efforts. The dominant political trend of the age fortifies the collective and technical organization of society. Freudian psychoanalysis reveals that the antagonism between instinct and civilization is founded on the more hopeless opposition between love and aggression. Existentialist philosophy exposes the absolute nudity of the self in a world devoid of preconceived values or significance. (*RI,* p. 20)

Against this modernist legacy Hassan proposes "to adapt the literary response to new conditions of survival," fostering a design for life which moves away from critical literalism in order to explore "the subjective life, the silent structure of language and of consciousness," all to implicate criticism in a wider experience, "the fantasy of culture" (*P*, pp. 27–28) in which these dead-end thoughts of modernism may be overcome.

When Harold Rosenberg faced the aesthetic problems of representational art, and when Roland Barthes encountered the difficulties of a bourgeois economy of signs which for its own profit naturalized the artificial, each found his best course of action not in a negative critique of the adversary system but in a re-visioning of the artist's and writer's activities themselves. For Rosenberg, painting is an act within the canvas's arena, and for Barthes *to write* becomes an intransitive verb, as opaque as its formerly signified objects. Hence it should be no surprise that in hearing the dire prophecies of modernism Hassan answers them not in their own critical terms but sets out instead to fashion a new language of criticism. His first concern is to recognize the primacy of vision in the arts, coming to terms with the spiritual force behind literary creation. For the critic this involves acquiring "an erotic sense of Style and an intuition of the New" (*RPF*, p. 13), for the important questions are ones of consciousness, and not just of literature itself. Mind affects our use of physical means, and so to reach that consciousness the physical must be part of the critic's repertoire. "Humanists must enter the sphere of active symbols now surrounding the earth," Hassan urges, "and bring to it what they know of language and the sovereign imagination. Humanists must enter the future. They must also dream" (*P*, p. 116). What the critic faces is not a coldly intellectual object but "a presence mediated cunningly, incomprehensibly by language," and he or she must be ready to reply in kind: "The work, that is, finally enters the total existence of a man, not simply his dream life or aesthetic consciousness; and in doing so it becomes subject to the total judgment of human passions" (*P*, pp. 6–7).

Hassan sees that the critic must do what the forward looking novelist has done: take an activist response which includes anticipating this change in the structure of consciousness and helping to effect it "by means of new fictions" (*DO*, p. 175). For the critic this involves an understanding of consciousness, particularly the way it is created by transgressing the very limits which first created it. Constraints are made and unmade, adding up to a self-transformation Dionysian in character, anticipating itself in an erotic opposite of nonbeing and ultimately bypassing language in favor of a general cosmic consciousness.

"Art is rehearsal for the orientation which makes innovation possible" (*LS*, p. 216), Hassan quotes Morse Peckham, adding that what is needed is an innovation in consciousness and not just in art. As with Rosenberg and Barthes, it is the restrictive terminology which must be discarded, the limiting paradigm of what criticism (like painting and writing) is that must be transformed: "What we call change is but the self-creation of knowledge; what we call future is but the virtual action of information upon itself; and language emerges as the feedback loop between cultural and biological evolution, accelerating, disrupting, both" (*RPF*, p. 167).

In Kafka's fiction, a new consciousness could be created simply by denying all our expectations—a deconditioning similar to that practiced by Ronald Sukenick, Frank O'Hara, and other novelists and poets who defamiliarize our world so that it may be seen anew (and thus *be* new). Conventionally literary language may no longer be able to carry this expanded sense of consciousness, and Hassan ponders the role expanding human thought will play. Any change assumes an order or a metaphysics behind it, he reminds us, and for him a new measure of consciousness is the central principle. One model of thought is the modern urban structure, where to see a city whole is "to apprehend its theoretical nature, its hidden functions, and ideal forms. For the city acts as mediator between the human and natural orders," and thus "enacts our sense of the future" (*CM*, pp. 95–96). Fiction does the same, reflecting the "crucial changes in American culture and consciousness" (*CAL*, p. 174) to which Hassan believes criticism must adapt itself. Models are available everywhere; it is up to criticism to comprehend them.

Changes in fiction are keyed to the "death of the novel" controversy, a debate which considers whether fiction's traditional forms are adequate to the new physical, moral, and philosophical conditions of postmodern times. That Hassan's critical development anticipates such innovation in fiction is clear from contrasting his reservations about 1940s and 1950s fiction in *Radical Innocence* with his appreciation of the entirely different style of work praised in *Contemporary American Literature*. In 1961 Hassan finds it ironic that a religious novelist such as Frederick Buechner cannot provide a vantage in his work from which a full account of human actions might be rendered; instead, this writer's characters falter in their inability to ascertain the facts. Hassan is equally surprised to see such self-professedly Promethean authors as Norman Mailer, William Styron, and Harvey Swados not only foregoing fictive heroism, but disallowing any protagonist the status of antihero—"no single eminence is accorded even to failure" (*RI*, p. 152). In similar manner Ralph Ellison is seen proposing a crisis of identity that cannot be resolved in any available terms, certainly not those of liberalism or romanticism; in Bernard Malamud's work, particularly *The Assistant*, there is a similar disinclination toward resolving matters, as "every act in the novel is whittled by irony, every motive is mixed with its opposite" (*RI*, p. 167). Ambiguity alone is the fate of any such hero.

Ambiguity, of course, is the modernist answer to questions of apparent meaninglessness, and Hassan sees his own disaffection with this response in the yearnings of certain transitional novelists. John Cheever seeks an answer in what Hassan calls the cartoonist's world, where a hearty gaminess allows a certain dream of immortality, even if slapstick in nature. What holds it together, however, is nothing in the novel's structure, but rather "a kind of unity in the marvelous state of mind the author wishes to impress upon us" (*RI*, p. 189). At least here is a sign of the emerging primacy of the author's imagination, a technical device in innovative fiction which Hassan's new thematics of mind anticipate. But fiction of this transitional era is still tied to representational conventions—the novel has not yet become an arena in which to act—and even as exuberant and form-eclipsing a work as J. P. Donleavy's *The Ginger Man* suffers from a plot which amounts to little more than a series of "gratuitous moments" (*RI*, p. 197). That the plot itself may be a gag suggests that fiction is moving toward an ironic consideration of not just its themes but of the novel's form, yet Donleavy's failure to capitalize on this (other than having style reflect theme) leaves Hassan with an art form considerably behind the consciousness of the times. Too often he finds novelists relying on juxtaposition instead of interaction, "ambience and verbal magic" instead of "dramatic resolution" (*RI*, p. 245). Salinger's form is often not aware of its purpose, and Bellow's philosophy (especially in *Dangling Man*) often fails to find an adequately sustaining form.

Perhaps the necessary forms for postmodernism's re-vision do not yet exist for the 1940s and 1950s fiction writer. This is certainly the case with Cheever's and Donleavy's attempts to champion the absurd, for which the comic form, with its pose of social judgment against absurdity, is inappropriate. When used nevertheless, it dissolves into a "frosty irony" (*RI*, p. 201). Better hope is found in *The Adventures of Augie March*, where the character's transformation happens on the level of style. Yet even here content inhibits the fiction writer's project, for the novel's exuberant style must "counteract the simplicity inherent in Augie's point of view" (*RI*, p. 310). The ideal would be to unfetter style from characterization, just as Harold Rosenberg's reformation of the canvas from a surface on which to represent to an arena within which to act frees the artist from the burden of presenting anything but his or her act of painterly creation. Such possibilities exist in fabulation, for this mode incarnates in its spirit the form of story-telling that takes language for its self-apparent medium. But in 1961 Hassan finds no writers on hand to sustain this fabulative style of fiction, and it will be 1967 before another critic, Robert Scholes, can describe in *The Fabulators* (New York: Oxford University Press) a group of writers who succeed on this level—and they, who include Kurt Vonnegut, John Hawkes, and John Barth, have no sufficient canon to be considered as early as *Radical Innocence*; once again, Hassan's anticipation of an "enfabled style" (*RI*, p. 227) is ahead of its time.

By 1972, however, he finds an entirely new world of contemporary American fiction. The action writing which Roland Barthes calls for in *Sur la littérature* is found by Hassan in the work of Ronald Sukenick, who "improvises himself even as he invents his characters, redefining both fact and dream." By dissolving the structures of identity, fable, and even of writing itself, Sukenick is able to take part in that revolution of consciousness in which "the supreme fictions of the mind constantly remake the forms of reality" (*CAL*, p. 171), a project in which Hassan's criticism shares. Both language and consciousness can be expressed in fiction, not through ironic comedy but by being made spatial entities in the novels of Rudolph Wurlitzer:

> People, pronouns, and places exchange their names, their identity. The sounds of words—Memphis, Omaha, Flagstaff, and so on across the nation—signify various states of futile awareness, states trying to coexist in the same mental space. As in Beckett's *Watt* or *How It Is,* entity supplants entity, voice blends into voice, fictions

unwind, nothing happens. Controlled maniacally, the language of Wurlitzer forces the novel to turn back upon itself, without distractions. (*CAL*, p. 173)

In similar manner Robert Coover's stories dislocate all causal relations of time and space, so that the creative self-consciousness of the author may be dramatized in the narrative's play.

This development in fiction is the most substantial correlative Hassan can find for the notion of change he wishes to suggest. The intellectual tradition offers him little on this point, for "We have no adequate, no truly contemporary, theory of change" (*P*, p. 152). Structuralism, even Barthes's, presents not change itself but rather codes, and Hassan dedicates himself to examining those codes to answer such questions as whether the Universe is given or still being made and the extent to which the mind itself is dynamic, change being intrinsic to its condition. But an examination of Paul Feyerabend's new philosophy of science and Thomas Kuhn's way of structuring new scientific revolutions shows that what has been assumed previously as a theory of change can be questioned on every count. It is not logic or evidence that promotes scientific innovation, these investigations show, but rather "ideology, belief, even accident" (*IR*, p. 23). Scientific arguments depend most of all upon certain *attitudes,* and changes in these arguments will encompass one's sense and scale of time, imagination and desire, interpretations of language, and the mind's action upon itself as a metaphysics is formed. The change that Hassan senses is underway involves a measure of Teilhard's *hominization,* for as human beings multiply, nature turns into history and history turns into "symbols, languages, traces of (im)pure mind" (*OE*, p. 35). The very notion of articulation is, at the end of this scheme, surpassed, and silence becomes an important element in Hassan's evolving critical consciousness.

Fascination with silence runs throughout the full body of this critic's work. Interestingly, his first mention of it is negative, because he finds it tied to a fictive expression still rooted in older terms of consciousness. If gesture is language, Hassan suggests, a writer such as J. D. Salinger will have devoted himself to a quixotic gesture which "defines the limits of his language and the forms his fiction takes." Because Salinger's gesture "aspires to pure religious expression—this is one pole—language reaches into silence." For a fiction writer, this is "a holy dead end," a self-defeating reaction against that other pole of gesture, the purely satiric one, which ends in sentimentality (*RI*, pp. 263–64).

Silence becomes a positive factor in literature when it embraces form rather than theme, creating the literature of silence Hassan celebrates in his second book. The form begins with certain refusals: Robbe-Grillet rejecting Sartre's humanistic pan-anthropocentrism, Henry Miller discarding the obsession for truth (and thereby transforming autobiography into an action writing), Samuel Beckett countering reason with a lively sense of absurd play, an aspiration to concreteness in the non-fiction novel, and in general the acceptance of chance and improvisation implicit in the refusal of order and purpose. Chosen instead is indeterminacy, whose form is "non-telic: its world is the eternal present" (*LS*, p. 13). These innovations may well be called anti-literature because of their basis in rejection, but those refusals are specific negations of themes and attitudes which inhibit the literary act, and in silence itself can be found a new positive value:

> Clearly, the silence at the center of anti-literature is loud and various. Whether it is created by the shock of outrage or of apocalypse, whether it is enhanced by the conception of literature as pure action or pure play, and of the literary work itself as a concrete object, a blank page, or a random array, is perhaps finally irrelevant. The point is this: silence develops as the metaphor of a new attitude that literature has chosen to adopt toward itself. This attitude puts to question the peculiar power, the ancient excellence, of literary discourse—and challenges the assumptions of our culture. (*LS*, p. 15)

By the time he writes *The Dismemberment of Orpheus*, Hassan is ready to argue that for nearly two centuries literary experiments "have tended toward vanishing forms. They carry intimations of silence, a consciousness spinning loose of history, trying to twist free of words and things" (*DO*, p. 247). Romantic dream may well have exploded words into outrageous visions, only to have Romantic irony move the imagination toward its abolition and persuade art of its own impossibility. Silence is the apt product of this long development, and Hassan is eager to draw its metaphorical implications: an avant-garde tradition of anti-literature, an alienation from reason, society, and history, a

Hollis Sigler, "She Wants to Belong to the Sky, Again," 1981. Collection of the Museum of Contemporary Art, Chicago. Gift of Illinois Arts Council Purchase Grant and Matching Funds.

**105
Ihab
Hassan:
Re-visioning
Man**

separation from nature, the repudiation of any art that aspires to the Romantic explosion into dream, the periodic subversion of forms in order to prevent any intimation of resolution or historical pattern, a creation of anti-languages which "transform the presence of words into semantic absences and unloosen the grammar of consciousness," an ability to fill recesses of the mind left empty by madness and mysticism, a turning of consciousness upon itself (altering the mode of its awareness), and finally a presumption of apocalypse, "the dissolution of the known world, its history and persistence" (DO, pp. 13–14). For some thinkers, such as Teilhard de Chardin and Norman O. Brown, the goal is a lost unity by whose standard all present languages must fail. For others, such as Sade, the "endless permutations of his ciphers are like the sexual permutations of his characters, ways of exhausting possibility and of achieving omnipotence" (DO, p. 28). In either case, there is a "terrible vengeance" which is turned against literature and language itself, whose previous forms of articulation are now seen as constraints. By releasing words from their associations, a window is opened on infinity. This is Hassan's description of Dada, but in its intention toward "the silence that divides life from death" Dada seeks "the line at which creation and destruction finally meet" (DO, p. 68), and so defines the goal of this new aesthetic.

The goal is not a negative one, and certainly not absurd or nihilistic as modern critics have claimed. "Must not life overwhelm art periodically," Hassan asks, "to insure the health, the prevalence, of man? Must not words aspire to silence?" (LS, p. 18). The classical forms of literature had been destroyed by the first Romantic artists who celebrated the indescribable, whose dreams defied material form. Here begins the making of "a literature without words—or to be more precise, a literature that disdains all but the most primitive and magical use of language" (LS, p. 22), a liberation from the constraining denotations that Hassan finds periodically necessary for art to maintain its vital function of inventing the real. When Henry Miller's *Tropic of Cancer* refuses to control or judge experience, it is employing a certain passivity of silence which allows what language that remains to face experience directly, without preconceived and delimiting structures which close off constructive possibility. There is no traumatic discovery in Miller's writing, no crisis of rebirth—"There is only the experience of flow" (LS, p. 63), for from this energy must come the new articulations literature provides for consciousness. Only a "concreteness of silence" (*LS*, p. 86) can yield such new vision. Miller's own vision is a state of cosmic innocence, Hassan observes, "wherein language ceases to intrude on our love. This is a vision of silence" (*LS*, p. 109).

In Samuel Beckett's work Hassan finds a different way of achieving the same effect, an "apocalypse by reduction" (*LS*, p. 113) which strips human consciousness of all previous forms of articulation so that its essential fraudulence becomes clear. By making consciousness a closed system, language is exposed as a game. Beckett dramatizes this condition by giving the mind nothing to think about except its own symmetry. Pure ratio, the zero degree of writing Roland Barthes seeks to read, is made the substance of Beckett's works, which are interesting and comic in effect because such rigid functioning "threatens the elasticity that social life requires" (*LS*, p. 134), just as Barthes's studies of bourgeois naturalization show. In Beckett's longer novels the narrative mirrors itself, proceeding in one direction only to turn back and reflect itself in the course of its own progress, another instance of system and ratio. His characters exist only because they speak; narration is a guarantee only of presence, not movement. Thus is created "the language of consciousness at its reflective task, the creative process giving phenomenological evidence of itself" (*DO*, p. 161)—the narrator having no identity apart from what he recalls or perceives: "*Malone Dies* brings a kind of poetic clarity to these verbal contrivances; at the same time, it shows a new purity of literal statement. Its inventories are but an example of the new way reason fondles a phenomenological world, which it is impotent to order. The result of such fondling is to transform objects into numbers in an infinite series and thus abolish the material world" (*LS*, p. 162).

Unlike American fiction writers of the 1940s and 1950s, Beckett's techniques of subversion are fundamentally structural; what theme there is "semantically abolishes itself" (*LS*, p. 173), just as in *Waiting for Godot* the only real death is of language. Within Beckett's art can be found a genuinely new form for the exercise of postmodern consciousness:

> The function of form . . . is to accept a basic intuition of chaos, and, paradoxically, to silence chaos in order to express it and silence language in order to express chaos. . . . Like Henry Miller,

Beckett understands that silence must be the ruling metaphor of the artist intent on discovering the form of chaos. Beckett, however, does not attempt to emulate disorder; he refines it into diabolical parody and in the process has evolved some of the most original works of our century. (*LS*, p. 208)

Yet there are American antecedents for the literature of silence, notably Ernest Hemingway's distrust of language, which gives his writing a reticence of understatement and a vocabulary "perhaps the smallest of any major novelist" (*DO*, p. 88). His linguistic terseness yields a structure in which small units follow one another invariably, as discrete events succeeding themselves without any attempt at synthesis and frustrating the reader's attempt to impose a greater meaning. The violence in Hemingway's vision compels a certain muteness, but Hassan reads in Hemingway's style more than just a reaction against the patriotic bluster idealizing America's role in World War I. Any words whatsoever belong to the public domain, and Hemingway's concern is the hidden world which requires a subliminal language. Citing a snatch of conversation which forms "the language of the death of love" in the story "Hills Like White Elephants," Hassan notes that "this dialogue may have been composed by Samuel Beckett," as the threat of oblivion "presses syntax into ineluctable shape" (*DO*, p. 100). Thus is silence not just a metaphor but the source of this writer's formal brilliance.

When consciousness exceeds the structure of literary language, silence may be an initial technique in reformulating that structure. The obdurate, threatening nature of objects in Beckett's fiction cry for silence; they literally deconstruct the characters' attempts to speak them. Silence itself then becomes a metaphor for any language which places itself in doubt, challenging the patience of humanists who feel that all is answerable to the image of man. Language can be denied in literature by many devices still couched in language: cancelling itself, deprecating its purpose, disappearing in the perspective of self-reflexive game, a random sense of ordering (such as Barthes's alphabet and the decentralizing impulse of semiotics), and the refusal of interpretation. Consciousness itself is created by transgression, and once articulated it "aspires erotically to its opposite: the void, nonbeing," toward silence as the limit "toward which language tends" (*RPF*, p. 37). In literature, silence begins as experiment, questioning itself through various forms of parody and subversion until it reaches the radical edge of speech, there to transcend itself wholly—in vain, Hassan reminds us, "for on the margins of silence, the dream of immanence teases literature, teases all art, back into waking" (*RPF*, p. 118). With all signs dispersed and consciousness fully extended, immanence becomes implicit.

A resistance to such immanence, rooted in a refusal to see the advantages of indeterminacy, characterizes not just modernism but its tenacity as a cultural vision. "When will the Modern period end?" Hassan wonders. "Has ever a period waited so long? Renaissance? Baroque? Neo-Classical? Romantic? Victorian? Perhaps only the Dark Middle Ages" (*P*, p. 40). Modernism's essential vision comprises an urbanism which puts Nature into doubt, a technologism in which city and machine cooperate in each other's construction, and a dehumanization in which elitism, irony, and abstraction rule, allowing style to take over. The aristocratic side of elitism fosters a certain fascism; irony encourages a complex play of formalism; abstraction leads to an impersonal reductiveness. All three express an "incipient revulsion against the human" (*P*, p. 50), simply because what the human implies has become unimaginable. Its authority rests on a certain elitist, self-generated order in time of crisis, most apparent in the posture of T. S. Eliot. Postmodernism confronts what modernism's paradigms keep at a distance, loosening fantasy from its objective correlatives and, to the extent that it privileges consciousness, anticipates a new Gnosticism—on which Hassan will speak at length.

There is a certain postmodernist will toward unmaking which disassembles the same modernist structures of authority which resist immanence and indeterminacy. This will expresses itself in a rejection of Descartes's cogito, and with this refusal of the traditional full subject comes a new affinity for fragmentation, fracture, and minority views. Claude Lévi-Strauss's structural anthropology unmakes Man as a coherent center; Roland Barthes unmakes literature and the book itself as a seat of authority, and removes the author as an originator; distinctions of genre disappear, while the unreliability of past forms leads to a distrust of all implied connections. Just as in Harold Rosenberg's de-definition of art, which Hassan cites in this context, there has been a "radical reorganization in our modes of knowledge, in the discourse by which we apprehend our very being—suggesting what Michel Foucault could call a postmodern *épistémè*" (*RPF*, p. 53). The evidence of our time for this change can be found in the new emphasis given choice, pluralism, fragmentation, contingency, and imagination, all under the rubric of indeterminacy; in the futurological interest in process and change; in the diffractions of the self, in which identity is variously lost, reunified in a Dionysian ego, divided, made protean, or deconstructed; in the displacements of desire which follow such reorganizations of the self; in the immanence of media, which shape our daily facts such as common reality has never been constructed before; in the unitary sensibility which marries religion and science, myth and technology, intuition and reason, popular and high culture, male and female archetypes, and ultimately earth and sky; and most importantly (and pervasively) the dematerialization of existence which makes fiction the primary resource of life. "Mind insists on encompassing more mind in itself, on apprehending more and more of reality im-mediately" (*RPF*, p. 111), Hassan notes approvingly, and finds such consciousness developing within the last reliable science:

> Even semiotics, science of all signs, sign of our times, opens itself to the full ambiguities of social reality and recognizes the continual shifts of semantic fields within a culture. Such shifts, despite the regularity of linguistic codes, can become creative, altering the rules of the semiotic game. Indeed, Umberto Eco perceives the semiotic project itself under the aspect of a kind of indeterminacy. The project, he says, "will not be like exploring the sea, where a ship's wake disappears as soon as it has passed, but more exploring a forest where cart-trails or footprints do modify the explored landscape, so that the description the explorer gives of it must also take into account the ecological variations that he has produced." (*RPF*, p. 114)

A refusal to accept this indeterminacy as a state of being characterizes modernism's reluctance toward the postmodern future. Contrasting the two, Hassan sees modernism as "essentially *authoritarian* in form and *aristocratic* in its cultural spirit," and the whole mood of indeterminacy (and of art which thrives on it) is foreign to its beliefs:

> Postmodernism, on the other hand, is essentially *subversive* in form and *anarchic* in its cultural spirit. It dramatizes its lack of

faith in art even as it produces new works of art intended to hasten *both* cultural and artistic dissolution. Orpheus is not only dismembered; his severed head seems to sing of sinking even as it sinks in the river Hebrus. Think of Barth's *Chimera*, Sukenick's *Out*, Federman's *Double or Nothing*, Saporta's *Composition No. 1*, Butor's *Mobile*, Cortázar's *Hopscotch*.

Hierarchic, ceremonious, complex, allusive, detached, the modernist authors, with their enormous technical inventiveness, still place the *forms* of art, the *artifacts*, between themselves and the self-parody, the consummate self-reflexiveness of postmodernists. The trend is toward the effective dematerialization of art, its conceptualization; the implied change is from the role of the artist as heroic maker to his role as absurd, and still cunningly heroic, player. Once again, this change is not simply chronological. (*JBP*, p. 193)

Of all the axioms which need to be redefined for modernism to make the transition to the postmodern, the structuration of One and Many, Other and Self is foremost, for here is the principle upon which modernism's Cartesian reluctance to reform the cogito with respect to indeterminance lies. Hassan's *The Dismemberment of Orpheus* looks back to Sade to find a world which the author has made his prison of consciousness. Orgasm shows the Self seeking to become the Other, but in Sade the result simply imprisons the Other within the Self. "All the ideas of Sade tend toward creating an absolute moral vacuum in the world," Hassan observes in a viewpoint which fits Barthes's notion of a language being made, "which he then proceeds to fill with his overweening consciousness" (*DO*, p. 37). Barthes calls it the making of a language, while Hassan prefers to see it as an "arithmetical" construction (*DO*, p. 39), but in each case fantasy is reduced to an equation. If man is orgasm, and orgasm is death, then the self sinks back into its own expiration.

A similar fate befalls Hemingway's vision. His quest for archetypal unity, revealing "a sacramental attitude that transcends any personal fate," explains the ceremonies of penance and propitiation that his heroes perform: "they are secret invocations of Being at its source. His redeemed characters know that the universe is not Naught but One" (*DO*, p. 92). But when that unitary sense of being diversifies itself too widely, the author's vision fails, and silence collapses into a garrulousness defaming author and protagonist alike.

A last resort of the Cartesian ego may be found in Kafka's *The Trial*, where the Self, in a last-ditch struggle, disappears completely, leaving only the Other. Kafka's despair over the otherness of reality is obvious, but his repudiation of the Self, as it is overwhelmed by the world, does not invite an acceptance of the Other. All definitions in this author's work are negatively phrased; style alone holds his world together, even in his posture of defeat. Yet as Hassan reminds us in a quote from Camus, Kafka's entire art consists in forcing the reader to reread, and the Other is at least envisioned in newly problematic terms. A certain dramatic economy and a talent for omission characterize this style, as they do Hemingway's—the movement toward postmodernism's silence is clear. In Cartesian terms, idealism is being reversed: by its uncertainty in dealing with the Other, the Self encounters a novel sense of doubt. "The rage for absurd analysis leaves no unity intact," Hassan observes, reminding us that as "all things multiply and are multiple" (*DO*, p. 119) under Kafka's scrutiny, indeterminacy and immanence become the inevitable state of affairs. Yet in Kafka's art there are no means for dealing with this state in positive terms: he offers a protest of spirit against matter, an "eternal prayer of self-transcendence" (*DO*, p. 121) which does little to envision an imaginable future.

With the nouveau roman, the reader is put in the same position Kafka holds as author: within the interior of vision, with just the surfaces of the Other to examine without any sense of penetration or understanding. The nouveau roman rejects character as a spurious psychological prop, just as Kafka has refused its humanistic benefits. But the situation is no longer dramatized as a product of art but presented as novelistic process in itself; the reading of a nouveau roman does nothing so much as give a phenomenological evidence *of itself*. There is no representation of the Other, only an assembly of the novel as Self in pursuit of itself. Yet Robbe-Grillet would seem to have created his own metaphysic within this structure, leaving nothing beyond the language he creates himself. For the literature which follows, there is no way out, Genet reducing himself to an object by submitting to the judgments of others, and Beckett's heroes locking themselves within the pure voice of subjectivity.

In the initial formulations of Romanticism, where Hassan finds the first step toward postmodernism, Coleridge unites the Many and the One. A century and a half later, a new equation is needed, forcing writers to rise to the cause: with conventional ideas of time, space, and character shattered, "The enormous volume of the World is matched by even greater expansions of the Self until reality becomes a declaration of the Mind" (*P*, p. 86), a circumstance Hassan finds equally true for the fanciful fictions of Rudolph Wurlitzer and for the nonfiction novels of William Styron, Norman Mailer, and Truman Capote. Since Hegel we have known that "what we call the self is but an active desire for the recognition of another, which the self sublates—at once negates and maintains—and so affirms its being, *for* itself" (*PB*, p. 594; *PMT*, p. 148). Hence the symbiosis of Self and Other in the nonfiction novel, that characteristic postmodern form which brings history into dialectical existence with the author, the person whose observation and participation make it happen as the form of his or her book. Yet the ultimate extension of this process is mystical:

> Whatever the self may be, its earthly form reveals a fierce intricacy of asseveration that no human endeavor escapes. Hegel and Nietzsche define a horizon of that being; in *The Varieties of Religious Experience*, William James defines another. James knows that "civilization is founded on the shambles, and every individual existence goes out in a lonely spasm of helpless agony." The insight is as stark as any Freud gave. Yet James knows as well the need of the self to risk itself at the edge of the ineffable. What he calls "the ontological imagination" realizes "unpicturable being" with a sensuous intensity exceeding a lover's ecstasy. Such a faculty overflows the self's finitude, and touches the moral and intellectual center of mystical experience. Thus the mystic or saint accedes to a higher type than the warrior or hero precisely because the former is more adaptable to "the highest society conceivable." Ethereal as James's speculations may seem to devoted realists, his major hypothesis stands solidly enough: mystics connect to something which, whatever it may be on its *farther* side, "is on its *hither* side the subconscious continuation of our conscious life." This is not far from Freud. (*PB*, p. 595; *PMT*, p. 149)

Is there a mystical element in postmodernism's acceptance of chance and improvisation? Such acceptance speaks against order, particularly the style of order imposed by rationality. Its silence is non-telic, seeking an eternal presence that indeterminacy allows. Objectivity is dismissed as a classically derived concept, while "Mechanism, determinism, materialism recede before the flux of consciousness, a kind of noetic Heraclitean fire." And since such an ideal structure of all potential structures is unrealizable, "knowledge must remain *finally indeterminate*" (*RPF*, p. 102). This state of affairs, Hassan insists, is optative, contingent, and manifold, sustaining many elements of our commonly accepted postmodern culture, including the pluralistic secession our society invites according to particular interests, the ecumenism and esotericism flourishing in religion, the freedom of the body from merely genital categorization, the rage for chaos as a biological mechanism countering the social drive toward order and resolution, the belief that science is essentially an anarchistic enterprise, variations in truth according to semantic fields, a tolerance of ambiguity tending toward asymmetry, the critic's new status as innovator, the blending of fiction and fact, the play of poetics and metaphysics in the view of historians, the toleration of opposites in postmodern architecture, and the indeterminacy of semiotics itself which sees semantics as continually on the move. "Where Arnold saw anarchy," Hassan distinguishes, "Foucault sees indeterminacies betokening another order of discourse" (*RPF*, p. 97).

The companion sense of indeterminacy, which shares its resistance of closure and celebration of ambiguity, discontinuity, heterodoxy, pluralism, and the like, is immanence, which Hassan defines as "the capacity of mind to generalize itself in symbols, intervene more and more into nature, act upon itself through its own abstraction and so become, increasingly, im-mediately, its own environment" (*DO-II*, p. 270). Language itself is based on the principle of immanence, and like Barthes Hassan finds it offers a good model for understanding postmodern thought. Such understanding welcomes an art which works "to delay closures, frustrate expectations, promote abstractions, sustain a playful plurality of perspectives, and generally shift the grounds of meaning on their audiences" (*RPF*, p. 116). As signs are dispersed, so does immanence become explicit in the farthest dispersal possible, the extension and expansion of consciousness. As nature is turned into culture "and culture into an immanent semiotic system" (*PPP*, p. 508; *PMT*, p.

172), a patina of thought lies on everything; a new gnosticism seems well at hand.

A "gnostic desire" to see the human condition as pure spirit pervades both Hassan's analysis of the postmodern condition and his own activities as critic. It is a "fantastic vision" which in its wish "to reform human consciousness even at the expense of its own art" does not merely revise literature but "trembles into language" as "the aspect of true spirit" (*CAL*, p. 21). This new gnosticism privileges Mind's ability to apprehend—and, indeed, the qualities of immanence and indeterminacy are better suited to a mental than to a materialist disposition. Matter itself becomes suspect, and anything in culture which derives from historical circumstance rather than from pure *logos* is regarded as accidental. Although such characterizations of mood have always been possible, the postmodern age is the first to possess a technology capable of placing such mentalism fully in play; consider the computer, which "promises by technology a Pentecostal condition of universal understanding and unity." From here it is a relatively short step "to bypass languages in favor of a general cosmic consciousness" (*P*, p. 122), a situation which may already be here, thanks to the will of our times toward the unmaking of forms:

> A certain dematerialization of our world is taking place, from the "etherealization" of culture (Arnold Toynbee) to the "ephemeralization" of substance (Buckminster Fuller) to the "de-definition" of art (Harold Rosenberg). The literary author "dies" (Roland Barthes), and the literary text vanishes into a generic abstraction, *l'écriture*. How many forms, disciplines, institutions, have we seen dissolve, in the last few decades, into amorphous new shapes? How many objects, solidly mattered, have we seen dissolve into a process, an image, a mental frame? "We are beyond space and time," John Brockman says in *Afterwords;* "we are beyond good and evil; there is only information; it is the control; the measure by which the operation of the brain changes. . . ." Dissolution again? (*P*, p. 123)

Hassan prefers a more positive answer: not a falling apart, but rather a remaking according to the new powers of consciousness, powers he considers syntropic—in the words of Teilhard, everything that rises must converge. Mankind's intellectual transactions take place with less and less intervention of matter, as hardware yields in importance to software and software recedes before pure mind. A physically decaying universe may well be regenerated metaphysically, as reality is dematerialized, nature is effectively transformed into culture, and culture expresses itself more easily in language and ultimately in consciousness itself. The process has been underway for nearly two hundred years, as Marx changed nature into an historical necessity, philosophers transformed culture into a set of symbolic languages, and Nietzsche established mental constructs as the primary resource of life. "Once a product of cosmic change, mind now finds itself prime agent of change in the cosmos" (*RPF*, p. 162), and Hassan relates it to the spiritualization of matter that was accomplished when the invention of the lens gave light new range and power. The only human order equal to this power of change is the mind, and as it takes its place increasingly among the operations of nature and history "Each of us, by virtue of Desire, Imagination, and Language, provides some awkward version of the Concrete Universal" which serves a unitary sense of purpose (*RPF*, p. 193). In the writer's terms, dematerialized existence is thus exploded into the play of logos, the universalist implications of which are implied in his concrete universalism, a humanization of the world which so saturates it with mankind's presence that it can be travelled just as we mentally explore ourselves. Citing Ernst Cassirer, Hassan notes that "Physical reality seems to recede in proportion as man's symbolic activity advances" (*JGM*, p. 187), and the challenge to mimesis that he finds so essential to the postmodern temper has its roots in "the active participation of the mind in 'reality'" to the extent that "mental intervention in nature" makes mimesis a never-ending, self-reflexive affair" (*WD*, p. 113).

The implication of science in this gnostic project is essential to Hassan's vision. "Science cannot be entirely free of faith or metaphysics," he asserts, because its advanced work constitutes an imaginative act: "The axiomatic basis of scientific theories cannot be extracted from sensory data; it must be freely invented" (*JGM*, p. 188). On this level the scientist is no more willing than the artist to merely confirm; dream, play, and poetry are more characteristic motives and modes of behavior in both affairs. All supposed facts are theory-laden; there can be no objective criteria for choice, since any such criteria are themselves obtained by theory. "The laws of myth and science have this in common: both are partial codifications of reality, ways in which the mind imitates itself" (*P*, p. 125); paradigms of science are metaphors which "delimit zones of thought and solve problems even as they generate new ones" (*RPF*, p. 157).

The overreaching mind is thus given preeminent position in Hassan's postmodern vision. No area of endeavor escapes it, from science to religion and art, and in this coincidence Hassan finds a figure to embody his quest. "Myth, Technology, and Literature meet in the various figures and fables of Prometheus," a role which represents "the creative principle of intelligence, creative yet essentially flawed because it is ignorant of its limit, its purpose" (*P*, p. 127). He soon modifies this talent to "the *right* Promethean fire," a power best expressed through women because "they eschew the latent madness of Prometheus. What madness? Pride, will, rootless intelligence, what every Ahab or Faust, vulgarly speaking, refuses to acknowledge" (*RPF*, p. xiii). These styles are quickly reflected in Hassan's view of both literary history and emerging form. For the organizational structure of *Contemporary American Literature*, he singles out key figures for the genres—Saul Bellow and Norman Mailer for fiction, Robert Lowell in poetry—and finds it significant that no contemporary dramatist can match the pre-war eminence of Eugene O'Neill. Bellow is noteworthy for being the first "to declare the promise of the new literature" (*CAL*, p. 27), while Mailer succeeds when he "finds his true voice, the right timbre and style of an apocalyptic imagination, the release of ambition" (*CAL*, p. 34). To be the era's "chief representative," as Hassan finds the fully formed Mailer, one must possess a "power to shape the moment" (*CAL*, p. 31), but it's only on a slightly lower level of Promethean endeavor that one sees Robert Lowell using autobiography as "the form of anguish or vulnerability by which the poet can engage the world" (*CAL*, p. 96).

The Promethean nature of autobiography is evident in Hassan's own tactics as a critic and writer. His style of "paracriticism," he explains, is a creative response, "an attempt to recover the art of multivocation. Not the text and its letters but metaphors thereof. Not a form strictly imposed but the tentativeness between one form and another" (*P*, p. 25). He makes creative use of his mistakes and misdirections, and when reviewing his choices for *The Dismemberment of Orpheus* finds it significant that though wanting to write about Blake, he chooses

Sade instead, and that his attraction to Lawrence leads him to Kafka, just as a preference for Mailer produces a chapter on Genet. Years before his paracritical experiments and two decades in advance of his own personal imaginative self-study (*Out of Egypt*), he is drawn to Henry Miller's disposition that "writing is autobiography, and autobiography is therapy, which is a form of action" (*LS*, p. 9). Miller's is not an attempt to understand his life but "to *live* it, live it over and over again" (*LS*, p. 30). *The Right Promethean Fire*, described in Hassan's subtitle as a study of imagination, science, and cultural change, is qualified in its preface as the fragment of an autobiography, alluding to Paul Valéry's belief that there is no theory that is not in fact a carefully concealed part of the theorist's own life story. On the first page of his autobiographical journal Hassan admits that "I wanted to approach Prometheus, but it was Faust, all-too-humanly flawed, who kept coming to mind" (*RPF*, p. 31).

Whether Faustian or Promethean, the stages of Hassan's critical career remark his inclusive, holistic method. Though drawing on French theory, he is careful to detach himself from such limits of method. "Subtle rhetoricians, materialists, the French only disconnect," he warns, and against the implosive force of poststructuralist thought proposes "a concept of literature that is also explosive: outward into gesture and performance, outward into action, responsive to change" (*RPF*, p. 56). His is the project of the Promethean consciousness, the forming of an orbic vision "in which the inner divisions of consciousness and the external divisions of humankind are healed and made whole—made whole but *not* homogeneous, healed but *not* rendered uniform" (*RPF*, p. 191).

Hassan's characterization of his own critical work as "the need of art first to doubt, then to subvert or transcend, its own forms and authority" (*CAL*, p. 18) is eminently Promethean in nature. His manner of supplying fire is to "try to find my voice in the singular forms that speculation and this postmodern age seem to require" (*JBP*, p. 181), violating older formal restraints of critical method "in the hope of bringing inadmissible evidence into partial evidence" (*RPF*, p. 4); by playing texts against texts, "voices against voices," he invites language to open up a new discourse, the intertextuality of which might articulate the previously unsayable (*RPF*, p. 16). The constraints of form, he argues, are unnecessary limits to the imagination—and it is the imagination which, in Hassan's view, "makes our future, *is* our fate" (*RPF*, p. xvi). *Everything which exists today was imagined long ago,* the motto Hassan takes from William Blake, is augmented by Ralph Waldo Emerson's belief that all Nature is metaphor, of which it is culture's function to recognize and science's duty to formulate in intellectual terms. Like Emerson, Hassan seeks to "remythify the imagination, and bring back the reign of wonder into our lives" (*PPP*, p. 516; *PMT*, p. 182); in his autobiography, this ability is seen as "Self-recreation: a sovereign fiction that yet enabled me to resist, even to remake, 'things as they are'" (*OE*, p. 6).

The ultimate remaking is of the human race itself, and just as Prometheus's theft of fire transformed human power to approach that of the gods, so does Hassan transform the cultural critic's role in terms he admits may be overreaching in style, yet in substance absolutely necessary for mankind's vision to be sustained:

> It may also be that I impose too large, too exorbitant, a task on the humanities; Prometheus does prompt us to zealotry. Such promptings are patently ludicrous, if not thrasonical. Yet to bring the humanities into the Party of Hope (Emerson) as well as that of Memory is also to overcome the fear, crotchetiness, defeatism that pervade our profession. Who has not become weary of the old humanist vision, its intricacies of remorse, its pinched piety and riskless chatter? Bergson believed the universe a "machine for the making of gods." I take this as a summons, which imagination and science deliver to the humanities even as we are delivered to our future. (*RPF*, p. xix)

"In dreams begin the responsibilities of men to become gods" (*RPF*, p. 169), Hassan believes with Norman O. Brown, and adds Susan Sontag's belief that in postmodern literature may be found "the wish to attain the unfettered, unselective, total consciousness of 'God'" (*P*, p. 93). If Man is indeed the project of becoming God, as Sartre phrases it, and if mankind's evolution is simply God becoming aware of Himself (Teilhard), then the world will become at last "only a realized will,— the double of man" (*RPF*, p. 173), another sentiment from Emerson.

Personally, Ihab Hassan posits life against death, confronting mortality as a stimulus to work. Beginning the Serbelloni Journal of *The Right Promethean Fire,* he confesses that "I had the sense, that spring, of my time somehow outrunning nature" (*RPF,* p. 127), and his diary from Cassis remarks that "Our windows . . . face South. I also face my fiftieth year. My hair has begun to thin. Just now I think: 'I have never felt better!' Then I recall Faust again" (*RPF,* p. 34). Death, whether challenged or accepted, remains "our radical transaction with the universe" (*RPF,* p. 137), and the risk of autobiography becomes the apprehension of oneself "in the very act of its flight from death" (*PB,* p. 593; *PMT,* p. 147). Language is based on difference and absence, and implies a negation or symbolic murder of the thing signified; yet the act of language eternalizes this desire for presence, memorializing death itself.

Hassan's procedure, then, is much like Fitzgerald's at the end of *The Great Gatsby,* as Nick Carraway stares out across the ruin of men's dreams, yet admiring the Promethean effort as "we beat on, boats against the current, borne back ceaselessly into the past." The radical innocence he finds in his first literary subject is sustained in its critical method, just as the examination of his own quest from Egypt to the United States prefigures his philosophic theme. "Wherever Atlantis may have been or will be," he concludes, "some say that the energy of American illusion helps to discover it—and to corrupt it" (*P,* p. 176). America and its literature have guaranteed the pursuit of happiness and insured that endeavor by rejecting the history of the world. It is this informing power of the mind Hassan adopts, believing with William Blake that America is indeed another portion of the infinite.

Five

The Postmodern Habit of Thought

Fragments are the only form I trust, a statement by a character in one of Donald Barthelme's short stories, has been taken as the aesthetic statement of an era, and the essence of Rosenberg's, Barthes's, and Hassan's innovations have found their most profitable expression within a mastery of such forms.

Their books are by nature fragmentary, covering broadly diverse interests and in many cases composed of previously published essays, introductions, and addresses. Except for the brief *Arshile Gorky*, Harold Rosenberg never wrote a full-length book; his oeuvre consists of essays, most of them prepared for *The New Yorker* and intellectual journals such as *Commentary* and *Partisan Review*, whose progress over a quarter century and through nine collections marks a body of thought which coheres in its development but which nevertheless is formed in units averaging just fifteen hundred to four thousand words in length. Beyond his twenty-five-thousand-word account of Gorky's work, Rosenberg's only extended commentaries are his introductions to catalogues of Saul Steinberg, Barnett Newman, and Willem de Kooning.

Ihab Hassan follows a similar practice in his own writing. *Radical Innocence* reaches back seven years to draw eight separately published essays into the larger work; and just as this and subsequent studies respond fluidly to a literary history in the making, so does his *Paracriticisms* survey more than a decade to see how his own critical form has changed and developed. The paracritical essay itself is a triumph of the greater holistic sense achievable by using fragments, as otherwise "inadmissible evidence" is employed through a manner of frame-change and slippage to expand the bounds of comprehension. Indeed, Hassan's talent at orchestrating so many as eight different voices in one critical performance (pretext, mythotext, text, heterotext, context, metatext, postext, and paratext, all of which debate one another) leads to an expanded critical dialogue, covering much more ground and entertaining a wider variety of responses than does the conventionally organized essay. His triumph of multiple form is *The Right Promethean Fire,* which interpolates four sections from two autobiographical journals among five paracritical essays treating Hassan's most intimate theoretical concerns.

The most various approach to an emerging postmodern aesthetic is found in Roland Barthes's work. Assembling his two dozen books means searching through almost as many areas of the library, as his subjects span the range of contemporary cultural activity and occasionally the classics: fiction and drama, but also the fashion system, popular mythology, international relations, photography, the self-constructed language systems of figures as diverse as Sade, Fourier, and Loyola, classical song, the discourse of lovers, the pleasures of the text, linguistics, semiotics, and himself. Like the closer methods of Rosenberg and Hassan, Barthes's life work speaks for the decentralized, inductive nature of his interest, and also his distrust of any authority which does not arise from the creative act and its materials themselves.

In the critical method of all three writers may be found the same aesthetic principles argued in their work. A typical essay by Harold Rosenberg reflects his own disposition toward the action he appreciates in art; never considering himself an art reviewer, he takes an unusual amount of time after a show's opening to view, consider, revisit, and eventually express this process in his writing, and often his essay is as much about his coming to terms with an artist's work as it is about that work itself. When attempting to define a movement, he is no less interested in the thinking process involved, noting from the start that such definitions never fit the deepest artists involved. This is the sentiment that begins "The American Action Painters," as collected in *The Tradition of the New*. His four-thousand-word essay is divided into seven sections, six of them subtitled and four graced with footnotes sometimes longer than the section itself. After admitting that his analyses will have to flatten out the steeper hills and valleys of this landscape, Rosenberg begins his argument by creating an ambivalence in the reader, a movement which will oscillate throughout the essay: is something new being created, or is American art just catching up with Europe? This question is kept deliberately unanswered, for even though Rosenberg rejects the notion that Americans are copying earlier modern art, he is just as adamant that no new school is being formed. By keeping his readers from settling on either alternative, he allows time for the true innovation of Action Painting—which is, after all, an entirely new way of making and looking at art—to be understood.

Precisely at this point of suspended judgment, Rosenberg introduces his notion of the canvas ceasing to be a surface upon which to represent and becoming instead an arena within which to act. Revolutionary as this idea is, its effect depends upon the disclaimer which immediately precedes it: that there is no new school, no published manifesto uniting the sentiment of these artists, but that "What they think in common is represented only by what they do separately" (p. 25), which makes Rosenberg's new definition something much larger than a school, a movement, or even a break from a specifically antecedent tradition. Instead, the whole notion of what painting is is at stake.

With the reader's field of comprehension cleared, the remarkably new nature of Action Painting can be considered in its full impact: image in mind yielding to materials in hand, intention becoming less important than surprise, and object (even that figured by form, color, composition, and drawing) mattering much less than "the revelation contained in the act" (pp. 26–27). This is the extent of Rosenberg's introduction to Action Painting's special aesthetic nature, and so that its revolutionary impact can be felt unhindered by other considerations he passes quickly to a section on its special quality of action. But there are other matters which he treats in an extensive footnote, drawing on a second essay, "Hans Hofmann: Nature into Action," which is not collected until *The Anxious Object*. Here Rosenberg explores the implications of that tension revealed in the painter's act, the most important of which is the art medium's being an extension of the physical world—not as a representation of something else, but material fit for enactment, making the action on the canvas *its own* representation: the painted gesture as sign, "the trace of a movement whose beginning and character it does not in itself ever reveal" (p. 27). This extremely Barthesean notion, however, is at this stage a deepening of Rosenberg's argument and not an essential development of it, and hence it is relegated to small print (albeit occupying most of the page). For the mainstream progress of his essay, the critic is anxious to establish action in painting as metaphysically identical to action in life, breaking down the earlier distinction and showing that the artist organizes emotional and intellectual energy the same as in a living situation. "Since the painter has become an actor," Rosenberg explains, "the spectator has to think in a vocabulary of action: its inception, duration, direction—psychic state, concentration and relaxation of the will, passivity, alert waiting" (p. 29). Sign and trace are important elements, but ones to be considered later. The essence of Rosenberg's present argument is to establish the new aesthetic of acting in art, and his essay's structure follows that imperative.

Next comes a consideration of art history and another possible disjunction, this time between socially committed artists who had been trying to paint political issues and those others (Cubists, Postimpressionists) who chose instead to paint Art. Again Rosenberg denies the effect of any polarity by eclipsing the question: "The big moment came when it was decided to paint . . . just TO PAINT. The gesture on the canvas was a gesture of liberation, from Value—political, esthetic, moral" (p. 30). Once again Rosenberg has suspended a potentially polarizing judgment to show that his ideal transcends the terminology of both alternatives, that a truly liberated art finds itself freed from whatever objects, social or artistic, are already in place. The end of Art signals the birth of the artist, just as for Barthes and Derrida the end of the Book means the beginning of writing.

Yet no sooner is this myth of self-creation explained than Rosenberg again forestalls another logical development, that of a mysticism surrendering to ritual. He accomplishes this by locating the Action painters' practice with regard to other styles within the American mystique, and by adding a footnote from his museum catalogue on the subject which emphasizes the role of decision inherent in this art. But even this concern is not enough to conclude his essay, for critical response and audience reaction have yet to be treated. In a final section addressed to these matters, Rosenberg's method reflects itself in microcosm, having cleared a path for his own assertiveness by suspending all possible judgments to the contrary:

> An action is not a matter of taste.
> You don't let taste decide the firing of a pistol or the building of a maze.
> As the Marquis de Sade understood, even experiments in sensation, if deliberately repeated, presuppose a morality. (p. 38)

Rosenberg's method, then, is shaped by the revolutionary nature of the new aesthetic he will propose.

A typical essay by Roland Barthes follows this same pattern of apparent digression and suspension of conventional judgment, again as a way of keeping the essential discussion alive until its transformation is complete. "The Eiffel Tower," from his collection of that title, shows this method at work, as the author situates his subject in a mental landscape and then surrounds it with the language of thought until its semiotic function becomes clear. As with Rosenberg, Barthes's method is not simply to explain but to enact, using digressions and abrupt shifts in perspective in order to put his play of signs into action.

As if to emphasize that his essay is less about an object than an activity which surrounds it, Barthes begins with a statement of absence squarely within the Tower's presumed presence. "Maupassant often lunched at the restaurant in the tower, though he didn't care much for the food: *It's the only place in Paris,* he used to say, *where I don't have to see it.*" Like language itself, the Tower pervades Paris, and Barthes admits that one has to take endless precautions about town not to see it. But when Maupassant speaks from its center, it is invisible to him—again, just like language. From this center Barthes moves outward, reminding us that as the Tower is seen from every neighborhood and in all types of weather, it becomes something whose meaning can be questioned forever but whose presence cannot be denied. It touches everything, even Barthes himself as he writes these lines, its silhouette framed by his window. As the paragraph proceeds and dusk falls, trying to conceal its existence, "two little lights come on, winking gently as they revolve at its very tip." Its presence connects the author to his Parisian friends he knows are seeing it, too. "With it we all comprise a shifting figure of which it is the steady center: the Tower is friendly" (p. 3).

This opening paragraph conducts the reader through the range of Barthes's own present situation: from the controversial nature of the Tower itself, through a graphic demonstration of its presence, to its effect on the author putting pen to paper with his subject not just in mind but in sight. Barthes talks about the Tower touching him and so uniting him to all his friends, but the mechanics of his vision have made the Tower touch us as readers, too, as it begins as an abstract statement couched in literary history and concludes this inaugural paragraph by intruding on the page we ourselves have now read.

Having moved his argument from the historical past to the most intimate present, Barthes now directs the reader's attention to the macrocosmic, for not only is the Eiffel Tower evident throughout Paris and within his writing (and our reading) act, it is universally present as the symbol of France. As an infinite cipher, standing everywhere for the French capital, it becomes the inevitable sign by which fantasies are expressed and realizations are confirmed. Meaning everything, it can be negated only by joining it to oneself, making this "only blind spot of the total optical system" one's own perspective (p. 4). With this accomplished, the Tower becomes a pure signifier, a form unceasingly placed upon meaning. As the occasion for a zero degree of writing, with no meaning or use by itself except as a repository of informed and applied opinion, it is a reminder that all meanings are humanly created. Neither a monument nor a museum, the Tower can be visited only so that one may participate in this projection of meaning: there is nothing to see *in* it, but everything to see *from* it. The experience it yields is a reading experience, for "The Tower looks at Paris. To visit the Tower is to get oneself up onto the balcony in order to perceive, comprehend, and savor a certain essence of Paris" (p. 8). From here things are seen in their structure; indeed, the Tower creates a structuralism by inviting an activity of the mind, decipherment. Finding things in their place is to imagine a history. Indeed, from it one can fancy that one owns the world.

Barthes's essay has taken the reader from the Tower to the page and back again, and in the process has made the reader a partner in the Tower's activity. Much like Rosenberg's essay on Action Painting, this piece on the Eiffel Tower suspends judgments and transforms polarities so that a new sense of appreciation may be formed; its deliberate fragmentation, jumping from Maupassant at lunch and friends scattered about Paris to Barthes at his writing desk and to the essay's readers placed atop the Tower, enacts the Tower's function at work, all as a way of putting the new aesthetic in motion. The extent of its range only points up the comprehensive nature of its concerns, for it is after all a language and not just a tower Barthes wishes to discuss. But it is by placing the reader inside the Tower's function, and making that function happen on the page, that the point is conveyed.

A similar kinetic effect is achieved in Ihab Hassan's essay, "Culture, Indeterminacy, and Immanence: Margins of the (Postmodern) Age," collected in *The Right Promethean Fire*. Hassan's paracritical essays give explicit form to the functional digressions and suspended judgments which characterize Rosenberg's and Barthes's best work. Originally relying upon metaphorical devices such as tape recordings, frames, slippages, anecdotes, and the like to signal variations within his printed text, Hassan restricts himself in this piece to what variations in typeface and layouts on the page can accomplish in terms of alternative expression. His argument is stated self-evidently at the start: that an episteme known as postmodernism is characterized by the play of indeterminacy and immanence. But there is also an admission of a counterargument: that these very qualities of the age make his own essay inconclusive, and that the bounds of rational statement restrict his access to their truth.

Does indeterminacy include anarchy? It does seem so when using an Arnoldian measure of culture, but Hassan finds that measure inappropriate to the American imagination which poses itself in an immanent future. Yet from the evening of Matthew Arnold's age come certain rumors, "chips and shavings of 1883–88" (p. 93) which Hassan can include as a series of fragments, brief sputterings of intellect as the Victorian age recedes, but the sum of which anticipates postmodernism: the decenterment of man, the vitality of the new, and any number of other features which by themselves may not be useful but once listed in the form fragmentation allows will anticipate Hassan's concerns. Take thirteen such statements from the declining age, parallel them with philosophical glosses (ranging from Emerson and William James to Norman O. Brown), and one achieves a Socratic dialogue with intellectual history yielding "the question of epistemes" (p. 96), Hassan's second topic.

Here Michel Foucault's notion of cultures being formed by systems of constraint helps distinguish the elements of Hassan's first question, which like Rosenberg and Barthes he has kept suspended until grounds for better judgment can be found. "Where Arnold saw anarchy," Hassan now counsels, "Foucault sees indeterminacies betokening another order of discourse" (p. 97). From here he reaches back to Einstein's principle that events are always perceived with reference to a certain frame; the only reality is that of field. Adding Heisenberg's Uncertainty Principle and Bohr's Principle of Complementarity blurs the ontological lines of being, and reveals that objectivity is just another fiction "transposed from classical concepts" (p. 101). With these new factors of science in play, Hassan can note that "Mechanism, determinism, materialism recede before the flux of consciousness, a kind of noetic Heraclitan fire" (p. 102). But as comprehensive as this argument is, there is still another matter which Hassan feels privileged to add as an excuse: "Gödel's proof that every logical structure is just part of noetic Heraclitean fire" (p. 102). But as comprehensive as this argument is, there is still another matter which Hassan feels privileged to add as excursus: Gödel's proof "that every logical structure is just part of a larger, stronger structure, with none ever being complete." Even the purest science thus seems more like a game of human invention than an objective discovery of reality, and all we have in the universe (thanks to quantum theory) is not a collection of physical objects but a web of perceived relationships. These concepts, Hassan believes, form a new cultural language, one that projects a new order of knowledge ments of the nineteenth century in decline and modernism not yet born.

The term *postmodernism* troubles Hassan, and he makes his discomfort with it a major part of his essay. Here he can allude to the general sense of moving beyond earlier concepts and regret that all we have is the notion of moving *beyond,* while the questions of beyond "what" and beyond "to" are never answered. Postmodernism is a movement in art, postmodernity is a movement in time, and Hassan wonders to what extent they coincide. Postmodernism in fact discovers affinities with art and culture from other periods, and is much more than just a rejection of modernist beliefs—the senses of linearity and belatedness implied by the prefix *post* are grossly inappropriate to the style of art and thought at hand. But to this objection, itself a digression in his essay, Hassan proposes another Socratic question whose maieutic form puts his argument back in motion: is this terminology just "a poor name for our desire, insufficient for the life we want to hold and bequeath?" (p. 109).

This question is answered by a wealth of evidence, so pervasive and comprehensive that Hassan needs no rhetorical device to shape its argument: all that is needed is an itemized list. Indeterminacy shows itself in cultural pluralism, fragmentation, and a multitude of choice; process and change rule the day; the once inviolate self glories in new diffraction, with desire happily displaced; media is everywhere, and religion and science intermix. Existence itself is dematerialized in a new immanence of mind, which Hassan enumerates in a twelve-item list spanning popular, artistic, and intellectual culture. These examples prompt another Socratic question: is not a new Negative Capability at hand, since postmodern man can be so capable of being "in uncertainties, mysteries, doubts, without irritable reaching after fact and reason?" (p. 115). That artists flourish in these circumstances is proved by Hassan's next section, which surveys the forms, techniques, and themes preferred by artists and writers of this era. All contribute to delay of closure, a frustration of what is expected, and the sustaining of a playful plurality of perspectives which characterize the postmodern aesthetic at its most pleasing. From all of this Hassan is lax to draw a conclusion, since postmodernism itself speaks against such rhetorical form. But he can note the circumstance of a transhumanized earth in which thinkers, like artists, can "mediate between culture and desire, history and hope" (p. 124). To do so is to learn to dream, which is Hassan's own paracritical quest.

The thoughts of Rosenberg, Barthes, and Hassan in action take the same form as their artistic theories espouse. When Harold Rosenberg argues for a new aesthetic of art as act, he guides the reader through a process of perception that dramatizes not just the painter's action on the canvas but the reasons behind that choice of expression which involve the viewer's own activity. Roland Barthes, for whom writing is an intransitive act, pertinent to itself, talks about the Eiffel Tower (or about any other cultural artifact) not as an object external to human activity but rather as the locus for the human systematics of language, especially as practiced in reading and writing. And Ihab Hassan's re-envisioning of humanity encompasses not just a description of the product but a rehearsal of its process as the mind expands itself to contain all that previously contradictory systems of thought have created. Common to all three is an appreciation that significance is not within the perceived object but within the activity of perception—not just in a conventionally idealistic sense, but in confidence that what defines the human is this process of surrounding the world with meaning, an act which their aesthetic uncovers and celebrates in its creative form.

Bibliography

All quotations have been taken from the first American editions of Rosenberg's, Barthes's, and Hassan's books and essays, except where a later edition (so noted) contains additional material or where a work has not yet been translated (in which case I quote the original version, make appropriate citations, and supply my own translation). Abbreviations used in the text precede each work below; an asterisk indicates that no abbreviation has been employed.

I. HAROLD ROSENBERG

AA	*Act and the Actor.* New York: World, 1970.
AE	*Art on the Edge.* New York: Macmillan, 1975.
AG	*Arshile Gorky.* New York: Grove, 1962.
AO	*The Anxious Object.* New York: Horizon, 1964; 2nd ed., 1966.
AP	*Artworks and Packages.* New York: Horizon, 1969.
ASM	*Art and Other Serious Matters.* Chicago: University of Chicago Press, 1985.
BN	*Barnett Newman.* New York: Abrams, 1978.

BNS   *Barnett Newman: Broken Obelisk and Other Sculptures.* Seattle: University of Washington Press, 1971.
CBR   *The Case of the Baffled Radical.* Chicago: University of Chicago Press, 1985.
DDA   *The De-definition of Art.* New York: Horizon, 1972.
DP   *Discovering the Present.* Chicago: University of Chicago Press, 1973.
*   *Steinberg: Le Masque.* Paris: Maeght Editeur, 1966.
SS   *Saul Steinberg.* New York: Knopf, 1978.
TN   *The Tradition of the New.* New York: Horizon, 1959.
WDK   *Willem de Kooning.* New York: Abrams, 1973.

II. ROLAND BARTHES

AC   *Alors la Chine?* Paris: Bourgois, 1975.
BR   *A Barthes Reader,* ed. Susan Sontag. New York: Hill and Wang, 1982.
CE   *Critical Essays.* Evanston: Northwestern University Press, 1972, translated by Richard Howard from *Essais critiques* (Paris: Seuil, 1964).
CL   *Camera Lucida.* New York: Hill and Wang, 1981, translated by Richard Howard from *La Chambre claire* (Paris: Seuil, 1980).
CV   *Critique et vérité.* Paris: Seuil, 1966.
EmS   *Empire of Signs.* New York: Hill and Wang, 1982, translated by Richard Howard from *L'Empire des signes* (Geneva: Skira, 1970).
ES   *Elements of Semiology.* New York: Hill and Wang, 1968, translated by Annette Lavers and Colin Smith from *Eléments de sémiologie* (Paris: Seuil, 1964).
ET   *The Eiffel Tower and Other Mythologies.* New York: Hill and Wang, 1979, translated by Richard Howard from *Mythologies* (Paris: Seuil, 1957) and *La Tour Eiffel* (Paris: Delpire, 1964).
FS   *The Fashion System.* New York: Hill and Wang, 1983, translated by Matthew Ward and Richard Howard from *Système de la Mode* (Paris: Seuil, 1967).
GV   *The Grain of the Voice.* New York: Hill and Wang, 1985, translated by Linda Coverdale from *Le grain de la voix* (Paris: Seuil, 1981).
IMT   *Image/Music/Text.* New York: Hill and Wang, 1977, edited and translated by Stephen Heath.
LD   *A Lover's Discourse.* New York: Hill and Wang, 1978, translated by Richard Howard from *Fragments d'un discours amoureux* (Paris: Seuil, 1977).
*   *Michelet par lui-même.* Paris: Seuil, 1954.
M   *Mythologies.* New York: Hill and Wang, 1972, translated by Annette Lavers from *Mythologies* (Paris: Seuil, 1957); essays not included here are subsequently translated in *The Eiffel Tower and Other Mythologies,* cited above.
NCE   *New Critical Essays.* New York: Hill and Wang, 1980, translated by Richard Howard from *Le degré zéro de l'écriture suivi de Nouveaux essais critiques* (Paris: Seuil, 1972).
OR   *On Racine.* New York: Hill and Wang, 1964, translated by Richard Howard from *Sur Racine* (Paris: Seuil, 1963).
PT   *The Pleasure of the Text.* New York: Hill and Wang, 1975, translated by Richard Miller from *Le Plaisir du texte* (Paris: Seuil, 1973).

RB   *Roland Barthes*. New York: Hill and Wang, 1977, translated by Richard Howard from *Roland Barthes par Roland Barthes* (Paris: Seuil, 1975).
RF   *The Responsibility of Forms*. New York: Hill and Wang, 1985, translated by Richard Howard from *L'obvie et L'obtus* (Paris: Seuil, 1982).
RL   *The Rustle of Language*. New York: Hill and Wang, 1986, translated by Richard Howard from *La bruissement de la langue* (Paris: Seuil, 1984).
SE   *Sollers écrivain*. Paris: Seuil, 1979.
SFL   *Sade/Fourier/Loyola*. New York: Hill and Wang, 1976, translated by Richard Miller from *Sade, Fourier, Loyola* (Paris: Seuil, 1971).
SL   *Sur la littérature*, avec Maurice Nadeau. Grenoble: Presses universitaires de Grenoble, 1980.
SZ   *S/Z: An Essay*. New York: Hill and Wang, 1974, translated by Richard Miller from *S/Z* (Paris: Seuil, 1970).
UT   "A Theory of the Text" and "Textual Analysis of Poe's Valdemar." *Untying the Text*, ed. Robert Young. Boston and London: Routledge and Kegan Paul, 1981, pp. 31–47, 133–61, translated by Ian McCleod and Geoff Bennington.
WDZ   *Writing Degree Zero*. New York: Hill and Wang, 1968, translated by Annette Lavers and Colin Smith from *Le degré zéro de l'écriture* (Paris: Seuil, 1953).

III. IHAB HASSAN

CAL   *Contemporary American Literature*. New York: Ungar, 1973.
CM   "Cities of the Mind, Urban Words: The Dematerialization of Metropolis in Contemporary American Fiction." *Literature and the Urban Experience*, ed. Michael C. Jaye and Ann Chalmers Watts. New Brunswick: Rutgers University Press, 1981, pp. 93–112.
CP   "The Culture of Postmodernism." *Modernism: Challenges and Perspectives*, ed. Monique Chefdor, Ricardo Quinones, and Albert Wachtel. Urbana: University of Illinois Press, 1986, pp. 304–23.
DD   "Desire and Dissent in the Postmodern Age." *Kenyon Review*, 5 [new series] (1983), 1–18.
DO   *The Dismemberment of Orpheus*. New York: Oxford University Press, 1971.
DO-II *The Dismemberment of Orpheus*, 2nd ed., enlarged. Madison: University of Wisconsin Press, 1982.
GS   "On George Steiner." *Salmagundi* No. 70–71 (1986), pp. 316–33.
IR   *Innovation/Renovation: New Perspectives on the Humanities*, ed. with Sally Hassan. Madison: University of Wisconsin Press, 1983.
JBP   "Joyce, Beckett, and the Postmodern Imagination." *TriQuarterly* No. 34 (1975), pp. 179–200.
JGM   "Joyce and the Gnosis of Modern Science." *The Seventh of Joyce*, ed. Bernard Benstock. Bloomington: Indiana University Press, 1982, pp. 185–90.
LS   *The Literature of Silence*. New York: Knopf, 1967.
MS   "Making Sense: The Trials of Postmodern Discourse." *New Literary History*, 18 (1987), 437–59; collected in *PMT*, pp. 191–213.
OE   *Out of Egypt*. Carbondale: Southern Illinois University Press, 1986.

P	*Paracriticisms*. Urbana: University of Illinois Press, 1975.
PB	"Parabiography: The Varieties of Critical Experience." *Georgia Review*, 34 (1980), 593–612; collected in *PMT*, pp. 147–66.
PMT	*The Postmodern Turn*. Columbus: Ohio State University Press, 1987.
PPP	"Pluralism in Postmodern Perspective." *Critical Inquiry*, 12 (1986), 503–20; collected in *PMT*, pp. 167–87.
Q	"Quest: Forms of Adventure in Contemporary American Literature." *Contemporary American Fiction*, ed. Malcolm Bradbury and Sigmund Ro. London: Edward Arnold, 1987, pp. 122–27.
RI	*Radical Innocence*. Princeton: Princeton University Press, 1961.
RPF	*The Right Promethean Fire*. Urbana: University of Illinois Press, 1980.
TP	"Timely Pleasures: Sane and In-Sane." Working Paper No. 5, Center for Twentieth Century Studies, University of Wisconsin-Milwaukee, 1985.
WD	"Wars of Desire, Politics of the Word." *Salmagundi* No. 55 (Winter 1982), pp. 110–18.

Index

Abstract Expressionism, 24–25, 32, 37, 45
Act and the Actor (Rosenberg), 24
Action Painting, 3, 7, 8, 10, 15–16, 18, 19, 22–23, 25, 28, 29, 32–33, 34, 35–38, 41, 43–44, 45, 47, 50, 54, 58, 68, 72, 78, 80, 87, 89, 94, 123–25, 127
Action writing, 87
The Adventures of Augie March (Bellow), 97, 101
Adventures of Huckleberry Finn (Twain), 94
"After Joyce" (Barthelme), 40–41
Afterwords (Brockman), 115
Ahab, 117

"The American Action Painters" (Rosenberg), 38, 123–25, 127
The Anxious Object (Rosenberg), 124
Arcimboldo, Giuseppe, 65–66
Argo (ship), 59
Arnold, Matthew, 114, 126, 127
Arshile Gorky (Rosenberg), 13, 16, 121, 122
Artaud, Antonin, 97
The Assistant (Malamud), 100

Balzac, Honoré de, 47, 79
Barnett Newman (Rosenberg), 15
Barth, John, 101, 111
Barthelme, Donald, 39–41, 49, 120

Barthes, Roland, 2–11 passim, 15, 16, 33, 34, 43–91, 93, 94, 95, 96, 98, 99, 102, 107, 108, 109, 111, 114, 115, 121, 122, 124, 125–27, 128, 129, 130
Beat literature, 38
Beckett, Samuel, 95, 96, 101, 103, 107–8, 112
Bellow, Saul, 97, 100–101, 117
Bergson, Henri, 119
Black humor fiction, 38
Blake, William, 95, 117, 119, 120
Bohr, Niels, 128
Bouvard et Pécuchet (Flaubert), 86
Brockman, John, 115
"Broken Obelisk" (Newman), 36
Brown, Norman O., 106, 119, 128
Buechner, Frederick, 99
Burroughs, William S., 38
Butor, Michel, 49, 111

Camus, Albert, 34, 81, 112
Capote, Truman, 113
Caro, Anthony, 35
Cassirer, Ernst, 116
Cheever, John, 100
Chimera (Barth), 111
China, 83–85
Clemens, Samuel L. (Mark Twain), 94
Cogito (Steinberg), 29
Coleridge, Samuel Taylor, 113
Coltrane, John, 38
Composition No. 1 (Saporta), 111
Conceptual Art, 37
Contemporary American Literature (Hassan), 99, 117
Coover, Robert, 102
Cortázar, Julio, 111
Critique et Vérité (Barthes), 86
Cubism, 16, 32, 35
"Culture, Indeterminacy, and Immanence: Margins of the (Postmodern) Age" (Hassan), 127–29

Dada, 7, 19, 106
Dangling Man (Bellow), 100

De Kooning, Willem, 3, 15–16, 17–18, 23, 25–26, 29, 36–37, 38, 41, 122
Derrida, Jacques, 15, 16, 124
Descartes, René, 109, 111, 112
Discovering the Present (Rosenberg), 15
The Dismemberment of Orpheus (Hassan), 8, 96, 103, 111, 117–18
Donleavy, J. P., 100
Dostoevsky, Feodor, 25, 94
Double or Nothing (Federman), 111

Eco, Umberto, 110
"Ecrivains de Toujours" (Seuil), 50
Eichmann, Adolf, 34, 35
The Eiffel Tower (Barthes), 46, 63, 73, 74, 83, 125–27
Einstein, Albert, 128
Eliot, T. S., 109
Ellison, Ralph, 100
Emerson, Ralph Waldo, 95, 119, 128
Empire of Signs (Barthes), 46, 67–68, 88

The Fabulators (Scholes), 101
Fashion, 51, 66–67
The Fashion System (Barthes), 51, 76–77, 88
Faust, 117, 118, 120
Federman, Raymond, 111
Feyerabend, Paul, 102
Fitzgerald, F. Scott, 120
Flaubert, Gustave, 69, 70, 71
Foucault, Michel, 26, 29, 109–10, 114, 128
Fourier, Charles, 69–70
Four Techniques (Steinberg), 29
Freud, Sigmund, 45–46, 113
Fuller, Buckminster, 33, 115
Futurism, 32

Genet, Jean, 112, 118
Giacometti, Alberto, 22
Gide, André, 55
The Ginger Man (Donleavy), 100
Ginsberg, Allen, 38
Gödel, Kurt, 128

Gorky, Arshile, 17, 18–19
Gottlieb, Adolph, 25, 32–33
Graham, Billy, 83
The Great Gatsby (Fitzgerald), 120
"Greyed Rainbow" (Pollock), 20–21 (illus.)

H (Sollers), 50
Haiku, 46, 58
Hamlet, 34
Handke, Peter, 97
"Hans Hofmann: Nature into Action" (Rosenberg), 124
Happenings, 37
Hassan, Ihab, 2–11 passim, 44, 93–120, 121, 122, 127–29, 130
Hawkes, John, 101
Hegel, G. W. F., 34, 113
Heisenberg, Werner, 128
Hemingway, Ernest, 108, 111–12
Hess, Thomas B., 39, 41
"Hills Like White Elephants" (Hemingway), 108
Hofmann, Hans, 3, 23, 24, 25, 26, 27–28, 29, 33, 35, 36, 37, 124
"Homage to New York" (Tinguely), 27
Hopscotch (Cortázar), 111
Howard, Richard, 45
How It Is (Beckett), 101

The Idiot (Dostoevsky), 25
Impressionism, 32
"The Italians" (Twombly), 60–61 (illus.)

James, Williams, 113, 128
Japan, 46, 48, 65, 68, 84
Jazz, 38
Johns, Jasper, 32, 33
Johnson, Samuel, 1
Joyce, James, 40–41, 49

Kafka, Franz, 99, 112, 118
Kerouac, Jack, 38
Kline, Franz, 32
Koch, Kenneth, 41

Krasner, Lee, 3
Kristeva, Julia, 48
Kuhn, Thomas, 102

Langer, Suzanne, 17
Lawrence, D. H., 118
Lévi-Strauss, Claude, 109
The Literature of Silence (Hassan), 95
Location, 39–41
A Lover's Discourse (Barthes), 76
Lowell, Robert, 117
Loyola, Ignatius, 62, 69, 70

McLuhan, Marshall, 24
Mailer, Norman, 100, 113, 117, 118
Malamud, Bernard, 100
Malone Dies (Beckett), 107
Malraux, André, 34–35
Marx, Karl, 34, 116
Le Masque (Steinberg), 26
Maupassant, Guy de, 125, 127
Michelet, Jules, 47, 50–51, 76
Michelet par lui-même (Barthes), 50, 51
Miller, Henry, 95, 103, 104, 106–7, 118
Mind, 98, 102, 110, 115–17
Mingus, Charles, 38
Mobile (Butor), 49, 111
Modernism, 6–7, 14–15, 47, 109, 110
Mondrian, Piet, 35–36
Monk, Thelonious, 38
Music, 38, 78–79, 89–90
Myth, 63–64, 72–73, 82
Mythologies (Barthes), 46, 63, 72–73, 74, 81

Newman, Barnett, 17, 18, 23, 24, 25, 27, 28–29, 32, 36, 37, 122
Nietzsche, Friedrich, 113, 116
Notes from Underground (Dostoevsky), 94
Nouveau roman, 46, 62–63

O'Hara, Frank, 99
Oldenburg, Claes, 35
O'Neill, Eugene, 117

"One (Number 31, 1950)" (Pollock), 30–31 (illus.)
On Racine (Barthes), 86
Orpheus, 44–45, 49, 111
Out (Sukenick), 111
Out of Egypt (Hassan), 118

Peckham, Morse, 99
Photography, 62
Picard, Raymond, 71, 86
Pollock, Jackson, 3, 15–16, 17, 18, 23, 25, 28, 29, 32, 35, 36, 38, 41
Pop Art, 27, 37
The Postmodern Turn (Hassan), 8
Prometheus, 117, 118, 119, 120, 128
Proust, Marcel, 47

Racine, Jean, 47, 62
Radical Innocence (Hassan), 96, 99, 101, 122
Rauschenberg, Robert, 28, 32
Redon, Odilon, 32
The Red Robins (Koch), 41
Reinhardt, Ad, 25
The Right Promethean Fire (Hassan), 118, 119, 122, 127
Rivers, Larry, 28, 33
Robbe-Grillet, Alain, 46, 49, 50, 62–63, 81, 103, 112
Roland Barthes par Roland Barthes (Barthes), 50, 51, 89
Rosenberg, Harold, 2–11 passim, 13–41, 43–44, 47, 54, 58, 59, 66, 67, 68, 78, 79, 81, 87, 89, 90, 93, 94, 95, 98, 99, 101, 109, 115, 121–25, 127, 128, 129–30
Rothko, Mark, 25, 27, 32

Sade, Donatien-Alphonse-François, Marquis de, 47, 69, 96, 106, 111, 118, 125
Sade/Fourier/Loyola (Barthes), 69
Salinger, J. D., 96, 100, 102–3
Sandler, Irving, 3

Saporta, Marc, 111
Sarrasine (Balzac), 79, 87
Sartre, Jean-Paul, 34, 103, 119
Saussure, Ferdinand de, 6, 59
Scholes, Robert, 101
Schubert, Franz, 89–90
Schumann, Robert, 89–90
Seurat, Georges, 35
Shakespeare, William, 34
"She Wants to Belong to the Sky, Again" (Sigler), 104–5 (illus.)
Silence, 108–9
Siskind, Aaron, 36
Snow White (Barthelme), 40
Sollers, Philippe, 49–50
Sontag, Susan, 119
Sorrentino, Gilbert, 39
Steinberg, Saul, 23, 26–27, 29, 122
Stella, Frank, 19
Stevens, Wallace, 39
Styron, William, 100, 113
Sukenick, Ronald, 39, 99, 101, 111
Sur la littérature (Barthes), 101
Surrealism, 7, 32, 37
Swados, Harvey, 100
"Synopsis of a Battle" (Twombly), 52–53 (illus.)
S/Z (Barthes), 79, 88

Techniques at a Party (Steinberg), 29
Teilhard de Chardin, Pierre, 102, 106, 115–16, 119
Thoreau, Henry David, 95
Tinguely, Jean, 27
Toynbee, Arnold, 115
The Tradition of the New (Rosenberg), 13, 33, 123
The Trial (Kafka), 112
Tropic of Cancer (Miller), 106
Twain, Mark (Samuel L. Clemens), 94
Twombly, Cy, 54, 78

Understanding Media (McLuhan), 24
"Untitled" (Twombly), 56–57 (illus.)

Valéry, Paul, 89, 118
Van Gogh, Vincent, 35
The Varieties of Religious Experience (James), 113
Vonnegut, Kurt, 101

Waiting for Godot (Beckett), 107
Warhol, Andy, 28

Watt (Beckett), 101
Whitman, Walt, 95
Woman (de Kooning), 25–26, 37
The Words (Sartre), 34
Writing Degree Zero (Barthes), 44, 81
Wurlitzer, Rudolph, 101–2, 113

Zola, Émile, 47

www.ingramcontent.com/pod-product-compliance
Lightning Source LLC
Chambersburg PA
CBHW011753220426
43672CB00017B/2949